Oppenheimer: A V ⸺ ⸺ ⸺

The interconnected stories of Robert Oppenheimer, Edward Teller and Lewis Strauss

David Boyle

For my two brilliant scientific friends, Amanda and Janet

"Those poor little people, those poor little people…"
Oppenheimer to Robert Wilson, before the bomb dropped on Hiroshima, July/August 1945.

"The atomic bomb really is in a sense the constellation of everything America stands for - both for what makes us great and for what makes us a problem in the world."
Composer John Adams on his opera *Doctor Atomic*, October 2008.

Chapter 1: Introduction

This is the story of three men, those who may have been most responsible for the development of the atomic bomb and then the hydrogen bomb, who were all deeply involved in the decisions that led to its use against Japan in 1945, but who ended up fighting each other in a secret hearing in Washington which has gone down in history as a notorious miscarriage of justice.

The former diplomat George Kennan, told his audience about Robert Oppenheimer at his memorial held in Princeton, New Jersey, that "there was nobody who more passionately desired to be useful in averting the caststrophe to which the devekopment of the weapons of mass destruction threatened to lead. It was in the interests of mankind that he had in mind here; but it was as an American, and through the medium of this national community to which he belonged, that he saw his greatest possibilites for pursuing these aspirations."[1]

Robert Oppenheimer was the father of the atomic bomb – and Edward Teller the progenitor of the H-bomb, who fell out spectacularly with Oppenheimer. Lewis Strauss was, by profession, a banker – but whose interest and involvement in nuclear policy, and whose capacity for hard work, led the US authorities to 'prosecute' Oppenheimer during the dark and febrile atmosphere of the McCarthyite era in the 1950s.

Ironically, they were all three of them born to parents with deep roots in Germany, Hungary or *fin de siècle* Vienna.

---

[1] Kai Bird and Martin J. Sherwin (2008), American Prometheus: The triumph and tragedy of J. Robert Oppenheimer.London: Atlantic Books, 5.

Chapter 2: Childhoods

Robert Oppenheimer's father, Julius, was born in Hanau in Germany, the son of a family of peasant farmers and mechanics. Julius came to the USA at the age of 17 in 1888. Both an uncle and an older brother had come ahead of him and he rapidly became a partner in his uncle's business, then he branched out on his own, importing linen and fabrics.

This was an immediate success. Julius married Ella Friedman, born in New York City – but also of German Jewish extraction – in 1903. She was an attentive and over-protective mother who taught music and after, she began collecting art. She was an early connoisseur to appreciate Van Gogh. This meant that her children were brought up with his paintings on the walls.

They named their eldest child Julius Robert, born on 22 April 1904 – but he was always known as Robert. Four years later, a brother – Lewis Frank was born. He only lived for six weeks. Partly because of that, and partly because he had been so prone to childhood illnesses, his mother always over-protected him. He was ever allowed to risk germs by buying from street vendors or to have his hair cutin a public barber shop.

Robert's communist friend Jean Tatlock said later: "You must remember that he was lecturing to learned societies when he was seven, that he never had a childhood, and so he is different from the rest of us."[2]

And he did. at the age of 12, he was using his father's typewriter to communicate with the well-known local geologists about rock formations in Central Park. Not realising his age, he was soon invited to join the New York Mineralogical Club, and soon after that they asked him to give a paper. His father was hugely amused

[2] Jeremy Bernstein (2004), *Oppenheimer: Portrait of an enigma.* London: Duckworth, 7.

and encouraged him to go ahead. When he arrived at the podium, there was a laugh from his audience because he needed a box to stand on. But he went ahead and read his paper, and he got applauded afterwards.[3]

His parents "adored him, worried him and protected him," said his cousin Babette Oppenheimer. But as he got older, his mother began to worry that he wasn't playing wth other boys of his own age.[4]

He was certainly a cosseted and lonely child. It may be that the relative opulence of his upbringing, in New York's Riverside Drive, next to the Hudson River, was a factor in why people got so cross with him in later life. Before he left school, he had studied six languages.

Julius was on the board of Felix Adler's Ethical Cultural Society, a non-denominational, non-religious church, with no prayers or ritual. As a Jewish boy, none of the schools near their then home at 250 West 94th Street would take him – so he went there.

The young Robert Oppenheimer suffered from a neurotic preoccupation "with self", and also with rock formations. "I was an unctuous, repulsively good little boy," he used to say.[5] He was shy and awkward, and had few friends.

His fortunes began to rise with the arrival of the science teacher, the 'marvellous' Augustus Klock. "I have a great sense of indebtedness to him," wrote Oppenheimer later.[6]

His brother Frank was born in 1912, just as the family was moving – together with their art – to 155 Riverside Drive. Robert had a tough, somewhat lonely childhood; during one summer camp at about this time, his parents complained to the organisers about teaching their son the facts of life. In response, they tried to ban dirty jokes. In retribution, the other children stripped him

---

[3] Bird & Sherwin (2008), 15.

[4] *Ibid.*

[5] Bernstein (2004), 10.

[6] Bernstein (2004), 11.

naked, painted his bottom red and locked him in the icehouse.

In 1921, at the frighteningly young age of 17, he won a place at Harvard, but he caught dysentery in Europe, so began his career in higher education in 1922, studying chemistry. After a year studying chemistry, he realised he wanted to shift to physics, he wrote to the physics department askng if he could take the higher level physics courses, mentioning the titles of 15 books he said he had read.

"Obviously, if he says he has read these books, he's a liar," said Professor Geoorge Washington Pierce when the committee met to consider his request, "but he should get a Ph.d just for knowing the titles."[7]

After he took his degree, he could have stayed at harvard, but instead he tried to get taken on as a pupil by Ernest Rutherford, the father of nuclear physics in Cambridge in England. His Harvard physics teacher, Percy Bridgeman, wrote recommending him, warning that "his weakness is on the experimental side. His type of mind is analytical, rather than physical, and he is not at home in the manipulations of a laboratory ... It appears to me that it is a bit of a gamble as to whether Oppenheimer will ever make any real contributions of an important charaacter, but if he does make good at all, I believe he will be an unusual success." Faced with this, Rutherford said no - but he passed his application on to J. J. Thomson, the man who had discovered electrons, and he agreed to supervise Oppenheimer.

By 1925, Oppenheimer was at Christ College, Cambridge, working in the famous Cavendish Laboratories, under Rutherford. "I didn't learn about quantum mechanics until I got to Europe," said Oppie. "I didn't learn about electron spin until I got to Europe. I don't believe they were actually known about in '25 in the spring in America; anyway, I didn't know them."[8]

Rutherford claimed to be one of only three people in the world who really understood relativity – the others may have been

---

[7] *ibid,* 33.
[8] *ibid,* 42,

Einstein and Niels Bohr in Copenhagen. In Cambridge, he worked with the physicist Max Born – also, strangely enough, the grandfather of Olivia Newton John. At that stage, Robert was working on the role of molecules in quantum mechanics.

Oppenheimer had something of a breakdown in England. From a mixture of isolation and home-sickness, and despair about the progress of his research. At one point in 1925, he made the great mistake of trying to poison his head tutor, Patrick Blackett, who had been hassling him to spend more time in the lab. Later, he claimed he had put cyanide into an apple, and left on his table - which was precisely how Alan Turing was to kill himself in England in 1954,

Whether he actually did exactly this isn't clear, but Blackett never ate it. Even so, the university aufhorities heard about it and Oppenheimer was in trouble. Luckily for Oppie, his parents were still in Cambridge and Julius Oppenheimer swung into action, persuading them to let his son stay - on condition he went to see a Harley Street psychiatrist regularly. He was diagnosed with *dementia praecox* – a version of schizophrenia that isn't used any more. In those days it was considered incurable.

Other incidenrs followed: he locked his mother in her hotel room in Paris and left, then he tried to strangle his friend Francis Fergusson, when he told him he was engaged to be married. "He was completely at a loss about his sex life," said Fergusson many years later.[9]

Again, luckily for Oppenheimer, he decided at that point to have a hiking expedition to Corsica with two friends. It was just what he needed. He also fell in love for the first time in Corsica. "It is known to few and they won't tell. You can't dig it out," he wrote later. "What you need to know is that it was not a mere love affair, nor a love affair at all, but love."

He met another girl in Göttingen, and spent much of his time paying court to her in what has been described a "formal, old-

---

[9] *ibid.* 47.

fashioned way."[10] The affair petered out back in the USA.

Even at a young age, 'Oppie' – the name his students were to give him – was tall and stooped, which made him seem a little fragile. He had piercing blue eyes and high cheekbones. His fingers and teeth were gradually going yellow with nicotine. He had wanted to be in Europe because that was where theoretical physics was developing fastest, yet he also took the time to master Dutch and Italian – enough to read Dante in the original.

In 1928, he joined one of the key European teachers, Paul Ehrenfest at Leiden University, then Wolfgang Pauli at Zurich Technical High School. Both men commented on the strange mixture of the depth and precision of his thinking and his rough and messy workings out. The truth was that Oppie was not a 'completer-finisher'. He was just too impatient – yet that applied to his own research: he found that, in co-ordinating a team, he could range more widely. He was awarded his PhD from Göttingen on the treatment of molecules in quantum mechanics in 1927.

If Cambridge was the centre of experimental physics in Europe, then Göttingen was the centre of theoretical physics.[11] What is more it was when Oppneheimer moved there, a majpr innovative period was coming to an end, including Heisenberg's matrix mechanism, Schrödinger's wave mechanics theory, Born's paper on probability and causality and Heisenberg's uncertainty principle. As Kai Bird and Martin Sherwin wrote: "by the time Robert left Göttingen the foundations of a post-Newtonian physics had been laid."[12]

In Born's autobiography, he wrote: "Oppenheimer caused me greater difficulty. He was a man of great talent and he was conscious of his superiority in a way that was embarrassing and

[10] Peter Goodchild (1980), *J. Robert Oppenheimer: Shatterer of worlds.* London: BBC, 211.
[11] Bird & sherwin (2008), 56.
[12] *ibid,* 57.

caused me great trouble…"[13]

He wasn't just a physicist either. This was a poem he wrote at around this time:

"Crossing
It was evening when we came to the river
with a low moon over the desert
that we had lost in the mountains, forgotten,
what with the cold and the sweating
and the ranges barring the sky.
and when we found it again,
in the dry hills down by the river,
half withered, we had hot winds against us.

There were two palms by the landing;
the yuccas were flowering; there was
a light on the far shore, and tamarisks.
We waited a long time, in silence.
Then we heard the oars creaking
and afterwards, I remember,
the boatman called to us.
We did not look back at the mountains."[14]

In 1929, Oppenheimer went to Berkeley to start a theoretical physics degree, and was then given a place on the staff there and at Caltech. During the summer before, he and his brother had rented a ranch in the Upper Pecos Valley, near Santa Fe.

"Hot dog!" he exclaimed when he heard it was available to rent. The owner said, since this is a Spanish speaking place, you should say "*perro caliente*!"

That was how his favourite place, eventually his own ranch, came to get its name.

---

[13] Bernstein (2004), 25-6.
[14] Bernstein (2004), 27.

**

By that stage, Edward Teller was just 21 years old and had just undergone the hiking accident that turned out to be so important in his life: he was in Munich, falling off a tram, when his leg was almost completely cut off at the ankle.

Teller was born on 5 January 1908. His mother doted on him and his Jewish father Max – an associate editor of the *Hungarian Law Journal* – was a self-effacing lawyer. Max had met Illona Deutsch at a friend's house in Budapest when she was 20 and he was 32. Sixteen days later, they were engaged.

In 1918, the Bolshevik Bela Kun emerged from a prisoner of war camp in Russia to take over in the newly independent Hungary. Soldiers moved into Teller's father's office, so that he could no longer practice law. Then, after 133 days, Hungarian forces under Admiral Horthy took over, and – just as Max had predicted – Horthy blamed the Jews for Bela Kun and he launched a reign of terror, executing 5,000 people for their role in the previous regime.

Most of them were also Jews. "Within my first eleven years, I had known war, patriotism, communist revolution, anti-semitism, fascism and peace," wrote Teller later. "I wish the peace could have been more complete."[15]

From the age of four, the young Edward Teller was obsessed with numbers. On one occasion, his younger sister Emmi asked over dinner why $(10+1)^2$ isn't the same as 10^2+1^2. And while Max tried to think about it, Edward knew immediately. It was clear that his son was extremely bright, which was why Max took him secretly to see his friend, retired maths professor Leopold Klug.

Edward's problem was how unpopular he was among his contemporaries – even with the maths teacher, who pointedly ignored him. He finally left the gymnasium in 1925, but his

---

[15] Peter Goodchild (2004), *Edward Teller: The Real Dr Strangelove.* London: Weidenfeld & Nicolson, 8.

mother, Ilona, believed that 17-year-old Edward was too young to leave home. He settled for a compromise, entering Budapest University to read chemistry. At the same time, he also entered the prestigious Eötvös competition, open to all gymnasium leavers across Hungary.

To everyone's surprise, he won the physics prize outright and the two maths prizes with two others. As a result, two weeks before his eighteenth birthday, he left for Karlsruhe in Germany to continue studying chemistry.

On the way to the exam, he had re-met Mici (pronounced *Mitzi*) Harkányi-Schütz, the younger sister of his friend Suki – who he had tutored in maths. His father had also encouraged him to meet some Jewish scientists, and one of these was the pioneering physicist Leo Szilard, who was to play a major role in this story.

His mother was worried about him and would have stayed in Karlsruhe with him – having searched out good enough butchers and laundry services for him – if his father had not ordered her home.

Two years later, with his father's permission, he went to Munich to study physics under Arnold Sommerfeld, a pioneer of the new physics. This was not a success: Sommerfeld was by then 60 and didn't welcome open discussion. In Karlsruhe, Teller had been a popular, if irritatingly condescending, figure. But in Munich, also, the accident would happen which would change his life. One day, he fell off the tram on his way hiking with friends. It nearly severed his foot.

Why did this have such an effect on him? Partly because it deepened his sense of himself as an outsider. But partly also because he became close to his surgeon, who disappeared while he was treating him (his father was the general who had frustrated Hitler's attempted coup in Munich in his beer hall putsch in 1923). So Teller went home and Mici came round every day to tend to him.

When he had recovered enough to apply, astonishingly, he was accepted by his hero Werner Heisenberg in Leipzig. Heisenberg was no Sommerfield. He was only six years older than Teller was, and the centre of a close-knit group of young people. In order to fit in, the 20-year-old Teller offered to make tea for everyone every morning. He carried on making it for two years.

Heisenberg was impressed by him. He set Teller a task about what became of the hydrogen molecule in higher energy states. This became his PhD thesis.

He travelled to Berlin at this time to hear Einstein lecture on unified field theory – a term coined by the great man himself – but he said he didn't understand a word of it.

He was, in fact, following in the same path that Oppenheimer had gone down five years before in Göttingen with Max Born – trying to apply quantum mechanics to understanding what happened inside electrons. Born and Oppenheimer had found it necessary to assume that the nucleus was motionless, and that the electrons around it are in motion all the time. Teller didn't accept that: he believed that the vibration and movement of a nucleus was vital to understanding what was happening. He asked his Hungarian friend László Tisza, one of the other Eötvös prize-winners to join him in Leipzig to find out.

But Tisza was a communist, and when he visited his home in Budapest, he was thrown into prison. Teller felt powerless and furious.

At the age of 23, the chemist Arnold Eucken asked Teller to go to Göttingen as assistant professor. There was to be no more marking essays for Heisenberg. During this period, he shaved his head rather than having to waste time in a barber's shop. Mici broke away for two years, studying in the USA.

Three years afterwards, in January 1933, Field Marshal Hindenburg appointed Adolf Hitler as Chancellor of Germany, and it was very quickly clear to Teller that there was no future for him in that country. From the moment the Nazis took power, no appointments were allowed without permission from the central government.

Within three months of Hitler's rise, the Academic Assistance Council had been formed in the UK, to help Jewish scientists come over. And so it was that the biochemist George Donnan asked Teller to come to London to work with him. On the way there, he met Mici in Budapest, took her to the countryside and proposed to her. She said yes.

They were married in February 1934 and took the train to Copenhagen, where he stayed with the great Swedish physicist Niels Bohr. Then in the Autumn of 1934, it was back to London and their small flat in Gower Street. Teller had fixed on nuclear physics as his specialist area when his friend, the Czech physicist, George Placzek, arranged a summer in Rome with the Italian physicist Enrico Fermi in 1932.

Mici Teller had been a student in Pittsburgh, and wanted to go back to the USA. Her chance came in 1935, when, thanks to George Gamow, Teller was invited to the United States to become a professor of physics at George Washington University in Washington DC, where he worked with Gamow until 1941. He was earning three times the salary he was getting in London.

There was no going back and they both became American citizens in March of that year.

It was not until 1937 that the two men – Oppenheimer and Teller – met for the first time, at a conference in Stanford University. They knew of each other's existence by then, and you could see why they might have hit it off. Both men had lonely, rather overprotected, childhoods. Both were gifted with a fascination for science, and both had made the shift from chemistry to physics in their twenties. Both had also gone, rather fearfully, to Göttingen and had enjoyed some success there. And later, after a period trying to apply quantum theory to chemical reactions, they had both come to the USA as professors.

Yet Oppenheimer was different, partly because of his family's wealth, and partly because he had been 'Europeanised' during the 1920s. When he began teaching at Berkeley and Caltech in California in 1930, he knew about wine, French medieval poetry and about European food. He could read Sanskrit, which he had taught himself as a way of understanding eastern philosophy.

He wanted to share all this with his students, to make every moment special. So, given that Teller was a sensitive soul, quick to take offence or feel patronised – and he was four years younger – you might easily imagine that they never got on well. And yet Teller was impressed: "I found talking with him very interesting

11

but dining with him was daunting. Before the seminar, he took me to an excellent Mexican restaurant with food so hot that I could swallow only a few bites," said Teller.[16]

Oppie's students adored him. Some of them took his course on quantum mechanics many times. One Russian woman was told she would not be allowed to take it for a fourth time, and went on hunger strike until she was allowed in.

With the help of Ernest Lawrence, the theoretical physicist behind the cyclotrons – equipment that accelerated atoms and fired them at an atomic target – the Berkeley physics department quickly became the largest of its kind for theoretical physics in the USA. Many of their graduates became professors around the world.

Oppenheimer also had a taste for risk and was a particularly dangerous driver – taking risks by racing trains. His Chrysler could go at 95mph. On one occasion, he crashed and a woman passenger was knocked unconscious. His father gave her a Cézanne drawing as an apology.

---

[16] Goodchild (2004), 40.

Chapter 3: The development of an idea

It was a devastating moment in human history, and also perhaps an age of relative innocence, which we can never recover. And the generation that gave birth to Oppenheimer and Teller were the ones working out what could be done about it – with a background of two world wars and a cold war in the century when they were born.

Oppenheimer, Teller and their contemporaries had been born in that moment of revolution, when innovations like electric light, cinemas, motor cars and telephones – plus submarines and air travel – were changing the way most people lived in the developed world. At the same time, a small group of scientists were also rethinking the accepted Newtonian basis of our understanding of the structures of life and the world.

If you were interested in ideas – and the young Oppenheimer and Teller certainly were – this was the moment to be born.

In fact, in Oppenheimer's first full year – 1905 – is sometimes described as Einstein's 'miracle year', when the great Swiss theoretical physicist published no less than four ground-breaking papers, which outlined the concept of relativity.

But then, even Einstein was standing on the shoulders of giants. Radioactivity had been discovered in 1896 by scientists Henri Becquerel and Marie Curie from working with phosphorescent materials. These glow in the dark after they are exposed to light, and Becherel suspected that the glow produced in cathode ray tubes by X-rays might have something to do with it.

So, Becquerel wrapped a photographic plate in black paper and put various phosphorescent salts on it. All the results were negative until he used uranium salts, which caused a blackening of the plate. This change agent was given the name 'Becquerel Rays'. It was soon clear that the blackening of the plate had nothing to do with phosphorescence. In fact, there had to be a form of invisible radiation that could pass through paper and was causing the plate to react as if it had been exposed to light.

DAVID BOYLE

At first, it seemed as though the new radiation was similar to the then recently discovered X-rays. But research by Becquerel, the New Zealand pioneer Ernest Rutherford, Pierre and Marie Curie and others, showed that this form of radioactivity was much more complicated. Rutherford was the first to realise that all elements like this decay in accordance with the same mathematical exponential formula. He and his student Frederick Soddy were the first to realise that many decay processes resulted in one element transmuting into another.

These early researchers also found that many other elements, as well as uranium, have radioactive isotopes. A systematic search for the total radioactivity in uranium ores also guided Pierre and Marie Curie to isolate two new elements: polonium and radium.

Marie and Pierre Curie's study of radioactivity was to be a vital factor in medicine – as well as building the Bomb. Their research launched an era of using radium for the treatment of cancer and the start of modern nuclear medicine.

While this had been going on in central Europe and the UK, in Basel in Switzerland, the young Einstein had been wrestling to reconcile the laws of classical mechanics with those of electromagnetic fields. Having decided they couldn't be reconciled; he began to develop his ideas about relativity. The famous equation $E=mc^2$ (E is energy, m is mass and c is the speed of light) expressed the truth that matter and energy were really just two sides of the same phenomenon. It showed that, if anyone ever worked out how to do it, it must be possible to create an enormous amount of energy from a very small bit of matter.

Einstein then extended the theory to gravitational fields, introducing his theory of gravitation in 1916. The following year, in 1917, he applied the general theory of relativity to model the structure of the universe.[17]

While Einstein was feeling his way towards the photon theory

[17] Peter Galison (2000), 'Einstein's Clocks: The Question of Time' in *Critical Inquiry*. Vol 26, No 2, Winter, 355–389, 377.

of light, other scientists were testing X-rays and finding that they could also burn people badly.[18] As early as 1902, William Herbert Rollins wrote despairingly that his warnings about the dangers involved in the careless use of X-rays were not being heeded, either by industry or by his colleagues. He had proved by then that X-rays could kill experimental animals – they could cause a pregnant guinea pig to abort.[19]

Ernest Rutherford, the New Zealand physicist who came to be known as the father of nuclear physics, won the 1908 Nobel prize for physics by discovering the concept of radioactive half-lives and the element radon. He did this at McGill University in Canada, but by the time he had won his prize, he had moved to Manchester University, where he came up with a theory that, although he could not prove that it was positive or negative, atoms have their charge concentrated in a very small nucleus.[20]

He performed the first artificial nuclear reaction in 1917 in experiments where nitrogen nuclei were bombarded with alpha particles. As a result, he discovered the emission of a subatomic particle which, in 1919, he called the 'hydrogen atom' but which, in 1920, he more accurately named the proton.[21] The year 1919 was when Rutherford also became director of the Cavendish Laboratory in Cambridge. Under his leadership, the neutron was discovered by James Chadwick in 1932 and – in the same year –

---

[18] K. Sansare, V. Khanna, & F. Karjodkar (2011), 'Early victims of X-rays: a tribute and current perception', *Dentomaxillofacial Radiology*. Vol 40, no 2, 123–5.
[19] Maria Rentetzi (2017), 'Marie Curie and the perils in radium'. *Physics Today,* Nov 7.
[20] M. S. Longair (2003), *Theoretical concepts in physics: an alternative view of theoretical reasoning in physics*. Cambridge University Press, 377–8.
[21] Ernest Rutherford (1920), 'Bakerian Lecture. Nuclear Constitution of Atoms', in *Proceedings of the Royal Society A: Mathematical, Physical and Engineering Sciences*. Vol 97, No 686, 374-400.

the first experiment to split the nucleus in a fully controlled manner was performed by students working under Rutherford's direction, John Cockcroft and Ernest Walton.

Rutherford died too early to see Leo Szilard's idea of a controlled nuclear chain reaction come into being. Even so, a speech of Rutherford's about his artificially-induced transmutation in lithium, printed on 12 September 1933 in the London paper *The Times*, was reported by Szilard to have been his inspiration for thinking of the possibility of a controlled energy-producing nuclear chain reaction. He had the idea while walking in London, on the same day. Rutherford's speech touched on the work of Cockcroft and Walton in 'splitting' lithium into alpha particles by bombarding them with protons from a particle accelerator they had constructed.

Szilard realised that the energy released from the split lithium atoms was enormous, but he also believed that the energy needed for the accelerator, and its essential inefficiency in splitting atoms in this fashion, made this impossible as a practical source of energy.

Rutherford died in 1937 of a hernia, and was buried in Westminster Abbey, near Newton and Darwin. Luckily, the Danish physicist Niels Bohr was on hand to take over the role of *eminence grise*. Bohr came up with the 'planetary' model of the atom, whereby the electrons orbit a nucleus – but where they can also jump from one energy level or orbit to another. The Bohr model has been supplanted by others long since, but its principles are still taught in schools. He conceived the idea of *complementarity* – that you could look at apparently contradictory properties of matter, both as waves and as particles.[22]

Bohr had founded the Institute of Theoretical Physics at the University of Copenhagen, now known as the Niels Bohr

---

[22] Don Howard (2004), 'Who invented the Copenhagen Interpretation? A study in mythology' (PDF). *Philosophy of Science*, Vol 71, No 5, 669-682.

Institute, which opened in 1920. Bohr mentored and collaborated with physicists from all over the world, particularly Werner Heisenberg. It was Heisenberg who introduced the idea that an electron could drop from a higher-energy orbit to a lower one, in the process emitting a 'quantum' of discrete energy. This became a basis for what is now known as the 'old quantum theory'.[23]

Heisenberg first went to Copenhagen in 1924, then went back again to Göttingen the following year, where he developed the mathematical foundations of quantum mechanics. When he showed his results to Max Born in Göttingen, Born realised that they could best be expressed using matrices. Heisenberg published his work in 1925 and, in a series of papers with Max Born and others the same year, the matrix formulation of quantum mechanics was elaborated.[24]

Heisenberg is known for his 'uncertainty principle', which he published in 1927. He also won the 1932 Nobel physics prize for "the creation of quantum mechanics".[25]

**

By that stage, Oppenheimer and Teller were both involved in the swirl of scientific debate, just as Oppenheimer's senior professor at Berkeley, Ernest Lawrence, was developing the cyclotron. This piece of equipment sped particles around so fast that they could almost reach the speed of light. It turned out to be crucial in the development of nuclear technology.

In 1931, Harold Urey at Columbia University in New York, isolated a new kind of hydrogen. Ordinary hydrogen has a single positively-charged particle, the proton. Heavy hydrogen has a proton and also a nucleus, called a *deuteron*. 'Heavy water' meant

---

[23] Emilion Segrè (1980), *From X-rays to Quarks: Modern Physicists and their Discoveries.* W.H. Freeman.
[24] Abraham Pais (1991), *Niels Bohr's Times, In Physics, Philosophy and Polity.* Oxford: Clarendon Press, 275-9.
[25] Werner Heisenberg on Nobelprize.org.

two deuterons bonded to an oxygen atom.

Five years before, in 1926, Oppenheimer had written the first paper about the tunnelling effect that matter has – under quantum theory, it is like a wave. That same month, Bohr travelled to Leiden in the Netherlands to attend celebrations of the 50th anniversary of Hendrick Lorentz receiving his doctorate. When his train stopped in Hamburg, he was met by the great physicists Wolfgang Pauli and Otto Stern, who asked for his opinion of the spin theory.

Bohr told them that he had concerns about the interaction between electrons and magnetic fields. When he arrived in Leiden, Paul Ehrenfest and Einstein informed Bohr that Einstein had resolved this problem using relativity. Bohr and his colleagues incorporated this into their paper. So, when he met Heisenberg in Göttingen on the way home again, he had become, in his own words, "a prophet of the electron magnet gospel".[26]

The year 1934 was an important one for nuclear physics. First, the Joliot-Curies in France bombarded a target with alpha particles and produced new elements in that way. Then later the same year, Fermi extended their work by bombarding elements, this time with neutrons. When he did that with uranium as the target, he found he had produced a number of radioactive elements.

When he was only 22, Fermi had been the first to point out the explosive potential of atoms that was represented by Einstein's famous formula:

"It does not seem possible, at least in the near future to find a way to release these dreadful amounts of energy—which is all to the good because the first effect of an explosion of such a dreadful amount of energy would be to smash into smithereens the physicist who had the misfortune to find a way to do it."[27]

[26] Jammer, Max (1989). *The Conceptual Development of Quantum Mechanics*. Los Angeles: Tomash Publishers, 188.
[27] Luisa Bonolis (2001), 'Enrico Fermi's Scientific Work', in C.

In 1938, he left Italy in response to Mussolini's racial laws, because his wife was Jewish, and he moved to the USA. He would also be vital to the unfolding story.

Bernardini & Luisa Bonolis (eds.), *Enrico Fermi: His Work and Legacy*. Bologna: Società Italiana di Fisica/Springer, 314–394.

DAVID BOYLE

Chapter 4: Enter Strauss

"In all likelihood I owe my life to decisions by three grandparents in the 1830s and 40s to leave Austria and Germany, and make their homes in the land of freedom."[28]

That was how Lewis Strauss (he pronounced his own name '*Straws*') began his 1962 autobiography, *Men and Decisions*. It is extraordinary how many of those most closely involved in developing nuclear weapons had family links to central Europe. One grandfather was in Franz Josef's army in Austria. The other one lost both eyes fighting for the Confederate side in the American Civil War.

It isn't irrelevant that, as Jews, they were aware and horrified about what Hitler was doing to their relatives. The thought of him with the potential of nuclear power behind him terrified them. Lewis Strauss was one of these.

The young Strauss was born in 1896, which made him a good eight years older than Oppenheimer. He began life as a door-to-door salesman until he was 20, in 1916, selling shoes, and he was good at it. By that time, he had savings of $20,000 – enough to go to college, and he was also reading everything he could about wave mechanics and radiation.

His great mentor was Herbert Hoover, then a mining engineer who had been asked by the US ambassador to London, Walter Hines Page, to help get Americans home safely when they had been stranded by the First World War.

Hoover had felt it necessary to advance his own money, relying on trust for repayment. Starvation in Belgium and parts of war-torn Europe, that he had seen while he had been there, inspired Hoover to greater efforts – and he, in turn, inspired women like

---

[28]Lewis Strauss (1963), *Men and Decisions,* New York: Macmillan,1.

Lewis' mother, Rosa Lichtenstein, to help collect clothes and to bag them up for starving Belgians.

Early in 1917, Woodrow Wilson asked Hoover to come to Washington to discuss more about starvation, given that there were now no surplus food resources in the UK. "When he gets there, why don't you go up and help him?" Rosa Strauss suggested to her son, Lewis.

So off went young Lewis by train to Washington, using his own savings, and he went straight to see their local senator, Thomas Martin from Virginia, who was happy to write him a letter then and there, claiming that he was a "valued friend of long standing". In the event, he didn't have the nerve to produce it.

He found Hoover in the new Willard Hotel. At least, Hoover arrived while he was in his office, wearing a hat and coat – and he agreed to Lewis' proposition that he could work for him for two months without pay. Hoover smiled and said: "Fine. When do you want to start?"

"Right now."

"Then, take off your coat," he said – and promptly left.[29]

By the end of the year, the Food Administration Organisation was fully staffed and working effectively. Lost cargoes from submarines reached a peak in April, making the impacts of the poor harvests in 1916 and 1917 even tougher, but Strauss thrived – and he never looked back.

He went to Europe with Hoover in 1918 in the *Olympic*, the *Titanic*'s sister ship. He also took charge of filling ships, anticipating the end of the war in November 1918, with food and bound for Hamburg and Bremen – but the victorious allies were not pleased. Hoover called their bluff and said the ships had been ordered to sail unarmed. The only way to stop them would be to sink them. As expected, the British and French navies let them pass.[30]

Hoover formulated a plan for feeding starving Russians during

---

[29] Strauss (1963), 22.
[30] Strauss (1963), 19.

their civil war and put the former Antarctic explorer Fridtjof Nansen in charge of it. Some of the food had been guaranteed by Hoover personally – about $500 million worth.

Then, at the age of 23, Strauss was suddenly asked to be comptroller-general of the League of Nations. He turned the job down on the advice of the great lawyer Louis Brandeis, who had telegraphed him: "Don't be a darned fool, love."

Instead, after the war, Strauss became a Wall Street banker, who left behind his links to Hoover – while carrying on supporting through his presidency until he died at the age of 90 in 1964 – and joined the bankers Kuhn, Loeb & Co.

Kuhn Loeb's major customers were railways, and by the mid-1920s, Strauss was helping to arrange financing for new railroad terminal buildings in Cincinnati and Richmond. His pay was enormous - $120,000 (equivalent to $1.9m in 2021).[31] Later, Strauss arranged the firm's financing for a number of steel companies and he helped bring Kodachrome film to market for Eastman Kodak and the Polaroid camera.

He married Alice Hanauer, the daughter of a Kuhn Loeb partner, in a ceremony at the Ritz-Carlton Hotel in New York City in 1923. He was made a partner in 1929, at the worryingly young age of 32, by which time he was earning over a million dollars a year.

So, while Teller and Oppenheimer were settled into their new roles as professors, Strauss was turning himself into an expert on nuclear possibilities. He never did go to college, which might explain his combination of charm and spiky rage. Those who were plunged into the academic world of physics – who, like General Leslie Groves, the head of the Manhattan Project, often used to find themselves battling a sense of inferiority. For a man like Strauss, who clearly had a chip on his shoulder, this was particularly tough.

---

[31] Richard Pfau (1984), *No Sacrifice Too Great: The Life of Lewis L. Strauss*. Charlottesville, Virginia: University Press of Virginia, 34-7.

**

Oppie was developing his academic career at Caltech, near Berkeley in California. "Robert finds it difficult to form proper relationships with equals," wrote a colleague at the time. "He could be respectful and deferential to one or two people like Einstein and he was very happy to have adoring disciples at his feet. Anything else, there were problems."[32]

His young, left-wing students copied his mannerisms. Yet something was still missing, according to the theoretical physicist David Bohm:

"He was a dilettante. He just would not take his coat off and really get stuck in. He'd certainly got the ability, but he hadn't got the staying power."[33]

Oppenheimer clearly had some growing up to do before he could become an inspirational leader. But everything was about to change for him – in 1936, he discovered politics.

---

[32] Goodchild (1980), 27-8.
[33] Goodchild (1980), 30.

Chapter 5: The politics of physics

In 1936, Oppenheimer met Jean Tatlock, who was consciously left-wing. She encouraged him to worry about the Spanish Civil War. The communists had set up the Popular Front the year before to co-ordinate these leftist causes, and – as the FBI would discover later – it was a tough job to distinguish hard-headed communism from trendy liberal-left hand-wringing.

Oppie and Tatlock made for a tumultuous relationship. Her father was a professor of French literature at Berkeley and was very right-wing. To make sure he carried on seeing Jean, Oppenheimer was – over the following year – involved as a member of the Friends of the Chinese People, the Academic Committee for Democratic and Intellectual Freedom, the Western Council of the Consumers Union.

Following in her wake, and newly political himself, Oppenheimer also helped set up a California branch of the Teachers' Union, where he met Haakon Chevalier, professor of romance languages at Berkeley. What he never seems to have done – unlike Chevalier and Tatlock – was actually to join the Communist Party.

It is true that he once went to a party meeting, in his brother Frank's home (Frank Oppenheimer joined the party that same year, in 1936). In those days, there was still racial segregation in the local swimming pool in Pasadena. There was a great deal to kick against.

It was hardly a happy relationship with Jean, though it carried on in some form or other for years, before she ended it. She used to disappear for months at a time, and taunt him about who she had been with. Oppenheimer was in love with her; she suffered from serious depression.

In August 1939, he met Kitty Puening, who also had ancestry in central Europe – in fact, she was niece of Field Marshal Wilhelm Keitel, the head of the German army, who was to be tried and hanged at Nuremberg for his role in the Nazi regime. She had been married three times already – at that time to a British doctor called Richard Harrison, and before him to a communist organiser who had been killed fighting the Nazis as part of the International Brigade in Spain.

She knew she was in love with Oppenheimer very early on. He invited her and her husband to his ranch, but Harrison was waiting to do some medical exams, so she went by herself. Then suddenly she was pregnant.

In November 1940, she divorced her husband and married Oppie. In May 1941 – six months later – their son Peter was born.

**

Meanwhile, Lewis Strauss was deepening his involvement in nuclear issues as his rage against the Nazis grew.

"The years from 1933 to the outbreak of World War II will ever be a nightmare for me," wrote Strauss after the war.[34] "And the puny efforts I made to alleviate the tragedies were utter failures, save in a few individual cases – pitifully few."

He signed up to 20 affidavits saying that he pledged his wealth to support a few miserable people so that they would not be a drain on the resources of the USA. "None of the people were personally known to me and in no single instance has my pledge ever required fulfilment in the twenty years that have since elapsed... But I might have done so much more than I did. I risked only what I thought I could afford. That was not the test that should have been applied and it is my eternal regret."[35]

By 1939, he was travelling backwards and forwards across the Atlantic, negotiating fruitlessly with the British government on a scheme – to be funded by wealthy Americans, including Hoover (who offered to go out and take charge of the infrastructure) – to send Jewish refugees from Europe to a new British colony, to be

---

[34] Strauss (1963), 104.
[35] *Ibid.*

carved out of what is now Kenya, Tanzania and northern Zimbabwe.

The British ministers were determined to send them instead to British Guyana, where the Americnas knew there was not enough fertile land to make it work. Still, in the end, Strauss and his backers succumbed to the inevitable and agreed to Guyana – but then the war broke out and it was too late.

He had dinner with the future French premier Paul Reynaud in Paris on his final visit in August 1939. He, his wife and his son had wanted to see some of the sights of Europe before war broke out again. "So do you have your family here?" Reynaud asked. "When are you planning to leave?"

Strauss said that he had two reservations, on both the *Ile de France* and the *Normandie.*

"If I were you, I would take the earlier sailing," said Reynaud. "There may be a scramble to leave in late August."[36]

Sure enough, Hitler invaded Poland on 1 September.

Back home, two physicists – Arno Brasch and the dynamic and demanding Hungarian Leo Szilard – asked Strauss to finance them to build a surge generator. Like a cyclotron, this could accumulate an electrical charge, which could then be aimed down a special tube at a target.

Both Strauss's parents had died, in 1935 and 1937, from cancer – and neither had been given any access to radium in US hospitals. This could be a useful and fitting memorial for them, he felt. As a well-informed amateur, he believed that a huge cyclotron could produce radioactive isotopes of various elements, by bombarding them with subatomic particles. Radioactive cobalt would have advantages over radium because it would be much cheaper and easier to produce.

Strauss asked Westinghouse to help, and in the end, most of the cost for the cyclotron came from the Rockefeller family.

**

[36] Strauss (1963), 119.

There is no doubt that Teller was an inspirational teacher. "I don't understand it, but I will explain it to you," he would say.[37] He was also determined to make his mark on his chosen subject. In 1937, the year he first met Oppenheimer, Teller predicted the Jahn-Teller Effect, which distorts molecules in certain situations. This affects the ways that some metals react, especially the colour of certain metallic dyes.[38] Like other people involved in theoretical physics in the USA, Teller and Gamow were excited at the prospect of a visit in January 1939 by Niels Bohr. Gamow phoned Teller during Bohr's visit and said: "Bohr has gone crazy – he says that radium splits!"

"Within half an hour," wrote Teller later, "I realised what Bohr was talking about."[39]

When the conference opened the next morning, Gamow broke the planned agenda and told the conference that Bohr had something important to say. What he said was that the chemists Otto Hahn and Fritz Strassmann had repeated Fermi's experiment from four years before by looking at the properties of two of the radioactive substances which they had produced. They found that, actually, they were producing radioactive forms of barium and iodine.

They couldn't understand why they had barium. But they were also working with Lise Meitner to find out.

Meitner was Jewish. She had been invited by Max Born to go to Copenhagen. Hahn had written to the Nazi authorities to ask for permission for her to visit, but this was denied on the grounds that she would probably not "speak well of Germany." So one night, towards the end of 1938, Hahn and his friends smuggled her over

---

[37] Goodchild (2004), 36.
[38] Hermann Jahn & Edward Teller (1937), 'Stability of Polyatomic Molecules in Degenerate Electronic States. I. Orbital Degeneracy'. *Proceedings of the Royal Society.* Vol 161, No 905: *220–235.*
[39] Goodchild (2004), 42.

the border into Sweden. She lived until 1968.

In Copenhagen, Meitner and her nephew Otto Frisch realised that they had fissioned the uranium atom. Over Christmas 1938, they designed an experiment to test Strassmann and Hahn's theory. If uranium atoms were really split, they would fly apart at great speed and it would produce an enormous burst of energy – and this ought to show up on a Geiger counter.

They told Bohr what they were planning as he boarded his ship for America – and they told him about their success when he was halfway across the Atlantic.

Meitner and Frisch believed their results could have been explained if the neutron had been absorbed into the nucleus, then splitting the nucleus into equal parts, which meant that the atoms were lighter than the original uranium atom. Under Einstein's formula, $E=mc^2$, a tiny amount of matter would be translated into a huge amount of energy.

Bohr stayed at Princeton with Einstein and stayed with Strauss too. Einstein also stayed with Strauss. "I wish I could discuss with you more closely the great prospects and possibilities of mastering the nuclear energy opened by the discovery of uranium fission," wrote Bohr to Strauss when he was back home again.[40]

Szilard wrote to Strauss also in early 1939, about Hahn's discovery in *Nature*. It could lead to peculiarly destructive bombs, he said. He asked if they could meet in New York and, meanwhile, he went to see Teller in Washington and Fermi in Chicago. "Since my return, almost every day some new information about uranium became available, and whenever I decided to do something one day, it appeared foolish in the light of the new information the next day," he wrote.[41]

It became clear, for example, that a rare isotope of uranium was capable of fission. It would have to be separated somehow from the more abundant isotope, which could take about 5-10 years. Fermi believed a chain reaction would be possible – if the neutrons

---

[40] Strauss (1963), 171.
[41] Strauss (1963), 173.

were expelled from a nucleus when it fissioned.

Fermi's theory was confirmed by a number of small experiments in American universities in the following weeks. Szilard had managed to wangle a loan for a quarter of a ton of uranium oxide.

Chapter 6: The Hungarian conspiracy

Szilard had been trying to organise a voluntary agreement not to publicise the nuclear findings, but the French ignored it on the grounds that the cat was already out of the bag. One leading scientist wondered out loud to Bohr whether they should be talking about such matters at all. On the west coast, Oppenheimer and colleagues read about the experiments in the newspapers and were incredulous.

Then his colleague Luis Alvarez repeated the Frisch-Meitner experiment and he knew immediately what it meant. Within a few days, there was a crude, theoretical drawing of a nuclear bomb on Oppie's blackboard.

Szilard had been hoping for funding from Strauss who – through his bank and on his own – was by then one of the main funders of nuclear research at the time.

Szilard had pursued Strauss and his wife, Alice, by train to his holiday home in Florida. On the way home, he left the train in Washington and called the Tellers.

Mici invited him to stay, though she very much preferred him not to. Szilard felt the bed and remembered how uncomfortable it was – and said to Teller: "God, I've just remembered sleeping in this bed before – is there a motel nearby?"[42]

Before he left, he sat on the edge of the bed and said to Teller: "You heard about Bohr on fission … Know what that means?"[43]

Of course, Teller did. The thought of Hitler getting his blood-stained hands on an atomic bomb along these lines was terrifying, which meant that it was this small group of physicists – many of them from central Europe, who really understood the issues there – who had begun to discuss not publishing their results.

---

[42] Goodchild (2004), 44-5.
[43] *Ibid.*

OPPENHEIMER: A WORLD DESTROYED

Bohr thought that it was a basic condition for science that you don't have results kept secret or tampered with. Like most senior physicists at the time, Bohr believed that it was probably impossible to make a bomb along these lines – because of the huge difficulties involved in getting hold of enough uranium-235 – the only isotope of sufficient purity available.

There seemed little chance that the German scientists would have failed to understand the implication of the Hahn-Strassmann experiment. Bohr reluctantly agreed to keep quiet. Teller was delegated to go and persuade Fermi, on the grounds that he was closest to him. Fermi agreed too – as long as everyone else stuck to the deal.

But of course, they didn't.

Frèdéric Juliot-Curie was married to Marie Curie's chemist daughter Irène – they shared the Nobel Prize between them – only the second married couple to do so (the first were her parents). They had been working together to find ways of identifying induced man-made radiation. For whatever reason, although he knew about the agreement in the USA, he went ahead and published their work on nuclear fission in the UK journal *Nature* at the beginning of 1938. It was followed by a second paper which said that fission was possible and it even settled on the number of neutrons released per fission – 3.5 were emitted. So, Fermi and Szilard began to prepare their new findings for publication too.

There was an immediate reaction to Joliot-Curie in Germany, where Carl von Weizaker was put in charge of nuclear research. On 29 April 1939, there was a secret meeting at the Ministry of Education in Berlin, where they decided to take over the stock of uranium across Germany and to get more from mines which had been taken in Czechoslovakia the month before.

Fermi and Szilard fell out in Washington over whether to use heavy water or graphite to slow the nuclear reaction down – as you would have to do to make sure the fission took place. Eugene Wigner and Teller went to New York City in the summer of 1939 to try and make peace between them. Szilard was refusing to work on his own experiments. It was the first of many major decisions that would need to be taken – how to slow the reaction enough for it to go 'critical'.

But even more important was to prevent the Nazis getting to the bomb first. What could be done? The only hope among the handful of theoretical physicists in the know was that they might prevent the Germans from getting hold of uranium from the mine in the Belgian Congo.

Teller was in New York that summer. So was Szilard, and Wigner was just down the railway line in Princeton, and so the three former Hungarians began to organise what has since become known, quite affectionately, as the 'Hungarian Conspiracy'.

They knew that the Belgians were mining uranium in the Congo. They also knew that Einstein, by then living in Princeton, knew the Belgian queen mother (he used to write her letters addressing her as 'Dear Queen').

Szilard didn't drive, so Wigner drove him to meet Einstein, who was fishing at Peconic Bay, on Long Island.

Einstein was by then 60 years old and was fascinated to hear about the recent discoveries "I never thought of that!" he said.[44] But he saw the implications immediately, and promised to help in any way that he could.

The Hungarians agreed that they needed to write to Roosevelt – and aware that Roosevelt identified Strauss with Hoover, they had to find someone else as a go-between. So it was that, at the end of July 1939 – a little more than a month before the Nazi-Soviet invasion of Poland – Teller drove Szilard to see Einstein again, where they produced a new draft letter in German, with Teller writing it all down.

By the time the economist Alexander Sachs, took the final text to Einstein and Roosevelt – he knew them both – war had broken out in Europe. Sachs handed over a 900-word summary of the letter he had written. Roosevelt read it through.

"Alex, what you're after is to see that the Nazis don't blow us up?" said FDR, succinctly. He called in his aide, General Edmund 'Pa' Wilson, and said: "Pa, this requires action."

---

[44] Goodchild (2004), 51.

By then, Germany had banned the sale of uranium from Czechoslovakia. The battle was on. Luckily, Edgar Sengier, who represented Congo mining interests, realised the importance of uranium. He identified 2,000 steel drums of uranium ore on Staten Island. He was later given the Belgian order of merit for his help.

By early in 1940, Roosevelt had decided to give the nuclear weapons project to the US Army Corps of Engineers. He also launched an Advisory Committee on Uranium. Sachs was a member, and so were the 'Hungarians', Szilard, Wigner and Teller.

In their first meeting with the army ordnance top brass to discuss budgets, they met some scepticism: "We're offering a $10,000 reward for anyone who can cause a deathray to kill the goat we have tethered to a post. That goat is still perfectly healthy," they were told.[45]

Others said it would be unlikely to work. But Sachs pressed on.

Teller made a proposal, offering to research with Fermi as a volunteer. He reckoned that enough graphite they would need to slow the reaction would only cost $6,000. Even this modest sum produced a tirade about how it wasn't weapons that won wars – it was morale.

In fact, it would cost over $33,000.

Wigner said that if the army really didn't require weapons to win wars, maybe they should look again at their budgets. Luckily, the general in charge laughed and said: "Alright – you'll get your money…"[46]

Szilard was furious with Teller after the meeting for the modesty of his request.

---

[45] Goodchild (2004), 54f.
[46] Goodchild (2004), 55.

Chapter 7: The British are coming.

On 10 April 1940, the Nazis overran Norway and Denmark. In London, at the Royal Society's offices at Burlington House in Piccadilly, that same day, the first meeting of the so-called MAUD Committee took place.

The committee remained secret for decades after the war – though Stalin was given a copy in 1943, by the so-called Fifth Man, John Cairncross. 'MAUD' was not, in fact, an obscure acronym. It was the name of Bohr's housekeeper in Kent when he was there.

Chaired by J. J. Thomson, the Birmingham University physicist, it divided the work into four teams at four universities – Birmingham, Liverpool, Oxford and Cambridge. The MAUD teams were even able to get hold of a small amount of uranium oxide from Belgium, via Edgar Sengier. Rudolph Peierls, Otto Frisch and Klaus Fuchs were part of the Birmingham team, though they were excluded from the MAUD committee itself, because they were technically enemy aliens.

The first report was drafted by Thomson in June 1941 and this was sent to the USA. They were surprised not to have a response, so they sent the Australian physicist Marcus Oliphant, who had been supervising Peierls and Fuchs, ostensibly to swap ideas about radar – on which he had been leading research – but actually to find out what progress was being made over there.

When, in October, the MAUD committee finished their work, their finished report provided a blueprint for a bomb. It began like this:

"We should like to emphasise at the beginning of this report that we entered the project with more scepticism than belief, though we felt it was a matter which had to be investigated. As we proceeded, we became more and more convinced that release of atomic energy on a large scale is possible and that conditions can be chosen which would make it a very powerful weapon of war.

OPPENHEIMER: A WORLD DESTROYED

We have now reached the conclusion that it will be possible to make an effective uranium bomb which, containing some 25 lb of active material, would be equivalent as regards destructive effect to 1,800 tons of TNT and would also release large quantities of radioactive substances which would make places near to where the bomb exploded dangerous to human life for a long period."[47]

**

Before the war, in 1931, the American chemist Harold Urey had discovered an isotope of hydrogen with an extra hydrogen atom – which he called deuterium. His mentor Gilbert Lewis very quickly created 'heavy water', where the normal hydrogen protons are replaced by 'heavy hydrogen'.

Why were the Germans quite so keen to capture the heavy water plant outside Trondheim, for example? What did they know?

The answer was that, because it was hard to irradiate – it absorbed neutrons – it was believed to be a vital way of controlling a fission experiment or a nuclear reaction. Fermi, who Urey helped to leave Italy and move to the USA, was to use graphite instead in famous Chicago experiment.

In November 1939, Stalin had invaded Finland. Strauss eventually asked Hoover whether he would guarantee more funds for Finland, to buy food so the Finns could buy arms. Bohr even gave his old Nobel gold medal to be melted down to help the Finns. Months later, they asked for peace terms – by which time Nazi troops had marched into Denmark.

Bohr had been helping refugees from Nazism throughout the 1930s. After Denmark was occupied by the Germans, early in 1940, Bohr had a famous meeting with Heisenberg, who had become the head of the German nuclear weapon project. Whatever Heisenberg meant to achieve – he claimed later that he wanted to ask his old mentor if he felt it was alright to carry out nuclear

---

[47] Margaret Gowing (1964), *Britain and Atomic Energy 1939-1945*. London: Macmillan, 384.

research in wartime – Bohr gave him the brush-off. But what Heisenberg had said sent him into a panic.

By 1941, the fear was that – when Hitler talked about 'super-weapons' – he meant an A-bomb. As it turned out, he meant his V1 and V2 rockets. But this, plus the visit by Oliphant, was enough to push the Americans to act. In June 1941, Roosevelt created the Office of Scientific Research and Development (ORSD), with his engineering advisor – and president of the Carnegie Institution – Vannevar Bush as director, personally responsible to the president. The Uranium Committee became the Uranium Section of the OSRD, which was soon renamed the S-1 Section for security reasons.

Cockcroft, who was part of the British mission under Sir Henry Tizard, reported that the American project lagged behind the British one, and was not going as fast.

Britain was at war and felt an atomic bomb was urgent, but the USA was not yet at war. Oliphant had flown to the USA at the end of August 1941, ostensibly to discuss the radar. He found that: "The minutes and reports had been sent to Lyman Briggs, who was the director of the Uranium Committee, and we were puzzled to receive virtually no comment. I called on Briggs in Washington, only to find out that this inarticulate and unimpressive man had put the reports in his safe and had not shown them to members of his committee. I was amazed and distressed."[48]

Oliphant met with the S-1 Section and told them that "we must concentrate every effort on the bomb and said we had no right to work on power plants or anything but the bomb. The bomb would cost 25 million dollars, he said, and Britain did not have the money or the manpower, so it was up to us."[49]

Two years had gone by since the original meeting with Roosevelt, but the Uranium Committee had only managed to

[48] Mark Oliphant (1982), 'The Beginning: Chadwick and the Neutron', *Bulletin of the Atomic Scientists*. Vol 38, No 10, 14-18.
[49] Richard Rhodes (1986), *The Making of the Atomic Bomb*. New York: Simon and Schuster, 373.

spend $50,000. Oliphant went to see Oppenheimer's colleague Ernest Lawrence at Berkeley to pick his brains. Lawrence then went to see James Conant, the president of Harvard University, the government scientist who the Uranium Committee reported to.

"Ernest, you say you are convinced of the importance of these fission bombs," said Conant. "Are you ready to devote the next several years of your life to getting them made?"[50]

Lawrence hesitated only a moment: "If you tell me this is my job, I'll do it," he said.

---

[50] Goodchild (1980), 46.

Chapter 8: Wars and rumours of wars

Conant and Bush went back and organised a meeting with Roosevelt on 9 October 1941, which turbo-charged everything else. Lawrence went back to Berkeley and began to shift his precious cyclotron into a machine to extract the uranium-235 isotope from raw uranium oxide. He also asked Oppenheimer to work out how much uranium would be needed for an explosion.

He worked out that it required about 100 kilograms. Any less and you couldn't rely on the neutrons hitting another uranium atom. Any more and the bomb might get to be a little unwieldy.

**

On 7 December 1941, Teller was driving with Mici for lunch with the Fermis, in the New York suburb of Leonia, and they stopped to buy some petrol. The attendant was a little preoccupied, listening to the radio and, when he came out to serve them, he told them that Pearl Harbor had been bombed.

"Where's Pearl Harbor?" asked Teller.[51]

December 7 was a Sunday. "On Monday, the laboratory was a changed place," he wrote later.[52] "Overnight, every trace of opposition to the war had disappeared. Everyone's commitment was now wholehearted, open and complete. The day before, I had inhabited a nightmare world of colossal dangers and uncertainties; now the world was full of problems that might have solutions."

Like the assassination of John Kennedy, everyone in the USA who was alive at the time knew where they were when they heard about the Japanese attack on Pearl Harbour and Hitler's fatal declaration of war.

---

[51] Goodchild (2004), 60.

[52] *Ibid.*

OPPENHEIMER: A WORLD DESTROYED

On the Saturday night (6 December), Oppenheimer was at a meeting of the Lincoln Brigade from Spain and he came home feeling disillusioned by the whole business of communism and the Spanish Civil War. "I decided I had had enough of the Spanish cause," he wrote later. "And that there were other absolutely more pressing crises in the world."[53]

**

Strauss had applied to join the US Navy Reserve back in 1925 and had been called up in February 1941. He had by then reached the rank of lieutenant-commander. He had wanted to go into intelligence, but was blocked, reportedly because the director of naval intelligence didn't like Jews. Also, because Strauss's contributions to the Jewish self-help organisations B'nai B'rith had aroused the suspicions of FBI director J. Edgar Hoover.

Instead, he had been assigned as a staff assistant to the head of the Bureau of Ordnance, where he helped organise naval munitions. He and his family had moved to Washington DC, where they lived in an apartment at the prestigious Shoreham Hotel.

On 7 December, he was on a rare visit back to New York City, and was wandering down Madison Avenue wondering whether to go back to banking. There was a group of people around a parked car, trying to hear the radio. "What's going on?" he asked.[54]

"Big news," the man shouted. "The Japs have just bombed Honolulu but we shot down all their planes and sank all their ships."

Strauss was promoted to commander early in the war, then by November 1943, he was a captain. He rose in rank and influence due to a combination of his intelligence, personal energy, and ability to find favour in higher places. Strauss's rigid manner

---

[53] Goodchild (1980), 41.
[54] Strauss (1963), 130.

DAVID BOYLE

managed to make enemies during the war as well, including a long-running feud with the chief of naval operations, Admiral Ernest King. Roosevelt particularly disliked him, so his 1943 promotion to rear-admiral did not happen.

 Through the war, Strauss took advantage of his ties in both Washington and Wall Street. He was learning how to get things done in Washington via unofficial back channels, something at which he would become an expert.

At this stage, in 1941, he had been assigned to the naval ordnance department, which he was delighted to find was in the former food administration building, where he had cut his teeth helping Herbert Hoover.

A few weeks later, Strauss was appointed General Inspector of Ordnance for the navy. It was an absolute gift for an able administrator because they were re-arming and there were "bottlenecks running out of our ears", according to one production expert.[55]

But before he had even met the Bureau chief, Admiral William Blandy, he happened to be at a Washington dinner party with the new secretary for the navy, Frank Knox. Strauss was always well-connected and the next thing he knew, he was writing him a memo about how they should consolidate all inspections in the navy.

Blandy heard about the memo and he wasn't pleased to hear that it had been written by a junior officer in his own department and Strauss was carpeted. "Haven't you had the word that you may not communicate with anyone senior to me other than through me? What have you got to say for yourself," he said.[56]

In the event, Strauss had very little to say for himself, knowing that he was in the wrong. Luckily, Blundy roared with laughter and said: "I happen to agree with everything you have written," he said. "But I wish I had known of it before you wrote it. I could have improved your case."

The next morning, his job was changed and he moved into the

[55] Strauss (1963), 132-3.
[56] Strauss (1963), 134.

nearest centre of power – as executive assistant to the bureau chief, Admiral Blundy himself.

He ended the war as a rear-admiral himself, but he wasn't the kind of admiral who went to sea. He fought the battle of ideas and resources in Washington and turned out to be very good at it. Although the Manhattan Project would be under the control of the army, the navy research department was – very quietly – thinking ahead about nuclear-powered ships, and were busy developing a process to separate uranium using thermal diffusion.

Chapter 9: How to build an A-bomb

By the beginning of 1942, Oppenheimer had been asked by the veteran physics professor Arthur Compton from Chicago to carry on working full-time on the bomb project. He was then working under Gregory Breit, a theoretical physicist working for the Uranium Committee, with the strange title of 'Coordinator of Rapid Rupture'.

Breit was completely obsessive about security. That made seminars difficult and not very informative.

Four months into the war, in the spring of 1942, Breit resigned suddenly in disgust, leaving the field clear for Oppenheimer to take charge of nuclear research. He began to look around for unused talent. This was the moment when he pushed through and expedited Teller's security clearance.

Teller had been desperately disappointed to be excluded from the efforts to build a bomb, which were now centred around Chicago. He had been told that he was not needed because the theoretical problems had now been solved. But he suspected it was because he and Mici were technically enemy aliens. So, it was a huge relief to him to be involved.

In great excitement, he arrived in Chicago, but found that nobody had thought about a role for him, so he worked with the Polish-American physicist Emil Konopinski – looking again at Fermi's suggestion that a fission explosion could also initiate a thermo-nuclear reaction.

This opened up a new possibility – because it did not involve getting all that uranium-235 together. He felt frustrated: because not all the X-rays were emitted at once, there could also be a fusion reaction. In fact, there was no limit to how big the explosion could be.

Finally, in the summer, Oppenheimer asked him to join Hans Bethe and a few others in Berkeley, to talk through the project as a whole. They met in an attic room above the administration building, behind a locked door – and only Oppie had the key.

You can see why Teller was excited. Deuterium, a heavy isotope of hydrogen, was easy to assemble in comparison to uranium, and 100kg of deuterium would be available by the autumn of 1943, and before 60kg of uranium-235. Meanwhile, the main group of researchers were trying to work out the size of the explosion of fission bombs, extrapolating from the massive explosion in Halifax, Nova Scotia in 1917.

MAUD had said that neutrons needed to travel about 10 cms and then back into the uranium. That is about 20 cms for the chain reaction to start.

As chair, Oppenheimer "showed a refined, sure informal touch," wrote Teller later. "I don't know how he acquired his facility for handling people. Those who knew him were really surprised."[57]

In fact, Oppenheimer was starting to curb his arrogance.

It was also Teller who came up with the biggest potential glitch of all – that setting off an atomic bomb could trigger an ongoing reaction that could set fire to the earth's atmosphere. Oppenheimer went to see Arthur Compton in his holiday cottage beside a lake in Michigan.

"I'll never forget that morning," wrote Compton later:[58]

"I drove Oppenheimer from the railway station and down to the beach, looking out over the peaceful lake. Then I listened to his story... This would be the ultimate catastrophe. Better to accept the slavery of the Nazis than to run a chance of drawing the final curtain on mankind. We agreed there could only be one answer. Oppenheimer's team must go ahead with their calculations. Unless they came up with a firm and reliable conclusion that our atomic bombs could not explode in the air or the sea, these bombs must never be made."

But Bethe checked Teller's figures and found a couple of

---

[57] Goodchild (2004), 66.
[58] Arthur Compton (1956), *Atomic Quest.* Oxford: OUP, 127. Quoted in Goodchild (2004), 67.

unjustified assumptions. "Together with new difficulties, new solutions emerged," said Teller.[59]

While he was in Berkeley that summer, Oppenheimer was invited to dinner by his communist friend Haakon Chevalier and their wives were there too. Oppenheimer talked in very general terms about how an atomic weapon needed to be developed.

Teller came too. He did not feel that Oppenheimer gave away any secrets, but he remembered it.

**

By the late summer of 1942, the 'S1' executive committee had been relaunched from the old Uranium Committee by Vannevar Bush by October 1942. It was clear that somebody needed to take charge of the whole effort. It was the choice of Henry Stimson, the venerable Secretary for War – and he chose Leslie Groves.

Groves had been responsible for building the Pentagon. He was also by then the oldest colonel in the US army. He desperately wanted an overseas command.

The Pentagon project, through the US Army Corps of Engineers, had put Groves in charge of a budget of $600m. He had also been building military camps across the USA. So, he was very reluctant to take on the task of building an atomic bomb – which at that stage was expected to cost no more than £100m. He accepted only when he heard that Roosevelt had asked for him personally. It helped that he was promoted to brigadier-general.

"God help us!" said Bush after they met in August 1942. Groves was blunt and ruthless, "the biggest sonofabitch I ever met in my life," said his deputy, Colonel Kenneth Nichols, "but also one of most capable individuals."[60]

In Chicago, Groves found himself irritated by the scientists and their customary caution. He decided, and – using his personal authority, pushed through – a commitment to try all of the three

[59] Goodchild (2004), 66.
[60] Goodchild (1980), 56-7.

main rival methods of separating uranium-235 from uranium oxide, or from the relatively useless uranium-238.

There was Lawrence's massive cyclotron at Berkeley. There was Urey's gaseous diffusion project at Columbia university. There was Fermi's team trying to make a chain reaction happen in Chicago. They would all get first priority – and so would plutonium, which was first isolated by bombarding uranium-238 with deuteron early in 1941, and which looked likely to be easier to produce that uranium-235.

Groves found the academics infuriatingly unhurried. "How much material do we need to make a bomb?" He asked a room full of scientists in Chicago, including Fermi, Szilard and Wigner. They did the calculations on the blackboard in front of him – making one mistake which he was able to point out.

"How accurate is that figure?" he asked when they had finished – and to his horror, he was told it was accurate to a factor of ten. It could, in other words, be ten times less or ten times more.

"There is one last thing I want to emphasise," he said before he left. "You may know that I don't have a PhD, Colonel Nichols has one, but I don't. But let me tell you that I had ten years of formal education after I entered college. Ten years in what I just studied. I didn't have to make a living or give time to teaching – I just studied. That would be the equivalent of about two PhDs, wouldn't it?"

Nobody spoke until the general had left. Then Szilard exploded: "You see what I told you," he said. "How can you work with people like that?"[61]

But Groves found that he could work with Lawrence and Oppenheimer. They gave him a clear view of the practical and theoretical possibilities, though he was depressed by the slow progress that the Berkeley cyclotron was making, separating and creating uranium-235.

---

[61] Stephane Groueff (2000), *Manhattan Project: The untold story of the making of the atomic bomb.* Lincoln: Authors' Guild Backprint.com, 30.

So, in October, he flew Oppenheimer to Chicago so that they could talk all the way back to Washington on the train. Oppenheimer suggested that the way forward was to end the compartmentalisation of the Manhattan Project by organising a single laboratory, isolated from the rest of the world, so that it would be possible to have secure conversations. It clearly could not work in an open lab.

Groves decided on the spot that Oppenheimer was right and that he should run the lab. Nobody else could be spared, after all, the cyclotron project at Berkeley would need Lawrence to stay there.

That meant taking a clear decision to protect him from the FBI, which had been watching him for the previous two years.

Oppenheimer and Groves narrowed down the list of possible places where they could build a laboratory somewhere out of the way, where the scientists involved in the project could talk freely. They narrowed it down to Los Alamos in New Mexico – where Oppenheimer loved the landscape – in a former boy's school, with just enough water and electricity for the existing population. Back then, Oppenheimer thought they would only need about 30 scientists. This was to be a serious underestimate.

In fact, although Los Alamos played a central role in the Manhattan Project, equal kudos needs to go to a number of private sector engineers who were persuaded by Groves to take on solving specific problems or building plants without knowing all the specifications, or often what they would be used for – and a breakneck speed.

Like Percival 'Dobie' Keith from Kelloggs, who formed the Kellex Corporation and took on a series of brilliant engineers from the oil industry.

Keith had to build the first gaseous diffusion plant (K-25), without knowing how to do so, on remote land near Clinton, Tennessee, which was to become Oak Ridge – not just the first working nuclear reactor (X-10), but also a massive electromagnetic plant (Y-12). He had to do this without knowing the specifications for the pumps they would need to build, aware that – although the pumps might work, the seal would prove very difficult indeed.

And, even if the seals failed – as they did – it would still need to be open and operating from the summer of 1943.

Or Walter Carpenter, the tough-minded president of Du Pont, who persuaded his board to take on the job of building a huge engineering works at Hanford in Washington state, for the Manhattan project, agreeing to a contract that paid their costs plus one dollar – because he did not want them accused of profiteering, as they had been after the First World War.

He also oversaw the building of the reactor for separating plutonium there (B reactor), and for operating it once it was ready.

Or Jim White, general manager of Eastman Tennessee, a subsidiary of Eastman Kodak, who operated the electromagnetic plants at Oak Ridge.

Groves was beginning to realise what an enormously expensive project he had agreed to lead.

This was in itself a massive undertaking. By March 1944, the plant would need to be supplied with more electricity than the city of Boston. Each of the five reactors there – primarily for producing plutonium – needed 30,000 gallons for the Columbia River next door, every minute. In the meantime, it was being designed by Chicago physicists Fermi and Wigner.

In Chicago, Arthur Compton remembered that the Westinghouse lamplighter division had been experimenting with purified uranium for making lamp filaments – mainly on the roof of one of their buildings in Bloomfield, New Jersey. He asked them to produce some more, which they did – aware that it was important, but not why.

In December 1942, in Chicago, Fermi and his colleagues were able to test the theory by using piles of graphite around a uranium core, to slow down a chain reaction. He had taken over an area under the squash courts at the university's Stagg Field.

Fermi had guaranteed safety, but there was still an emergency squad in case he lost control, ready to pour liquid cadmium on top of the pile. Once the pile went critical, doubling neutron activity every minute, a calm Fermi was taking notes, quietly pleased to have been proved correct. The reaction was self-sustaining. Wigner unveiled a bottle of chianti and a delighted Fermi poured a little out for everyone in paper cups.

Compton called Conant and told him: "You'll be interested to know that the Italian navigator has just landed in the new world. He arrived earlier than he was expected."

"Were the natives friendly?" asked Conant.

"Everyone landed safe and happy," said Compton.[62]

**

Granville 'Slim' Read was the manager of Gil Church, Du Pont's man on the spot for building Hanford. Groves had known him for some time, and liked and respected him, and his hard-boiled approach.

On his occasional visits to the site, he would gather the contracting managers and engineers around him and say: "The major problem in building these plants is that we only have one chance. It's got to be right *first* time. A reactor is not like an automobile – if a car doesn't work, take it apart and fix it. But here, you won't get a second chance."[63]

Reporting directly to Groves, Colonel Franklin Matthias was the military commander of the Hanford operation. He and Church had to persuade the army, navy and air force chiefs of staff to give up their plans to train bomber pilots in the area – without being able to say any more than it was the most important project of the war.

When he had moved there, in March 1943, Groves told Church to brief all the local newspaper editors and politicians that they should not mention the site without talking to him first.

The next problem was that they needed a labour force of 45,000 workers – just when every industry was begging for manpower. More than 100 recruiters were employed, who hit new towns every day – everywhere except in Tennessee or New Mexico, in case anyone suspected there was any connection between Hanford, Oak Ridge and Los Alamos.

---

[62] Groueff (2000), 89.
[63] Groueff (2000), 139,

Soon they had gathered 11,000 major pieces of construction equipment to build 368 miles of roads for the new city, using 40,000 tons of steel, 780,000 cubic yards of concrete. The construction camp alone included 1,177 buildings, and reached a peak population of 45,000 people – plus 6,000 wives and children.

In March 1943, the same month that Gil Church arrived at Hanford, there was a problem with the nickel they needed to electroplate the inside of the pipework, to protect it from the corrosive properties of uranium hexafluoride. Groves, Nichols and Keith went to see K. T. Keller, the driven president of Chrysler, who agreed to take it on – aware that he trusted Groves, though nobody knew how the diffusers were going to work.

Carl Heussner, head of their plating factory, said that it could not be done – you could not plate nickel in such a way that it could stand up to that much punishment.

"Doctor," said Keller. "I know I did stick my neck out, but let me tell you why I did it. It was only because of my confidence in you. I know you're the man who can do it – will you try?"[64]

"I'll try," he said. "But what I have in mind will cost a lot of money. And that's just to try. There is no guarantee…"

"Well, doctor, what do you think it will cost?"

Heussner said that it might cost around $45,000.

Keller replied: "I'm making $75,000 available to you now."[65]

The problem of electroplating the pipes with nickel was solved by Heussner within weeks.

Even more difficult was the membrane barrier for the gaseous diffusion plant, which also almost defeated them. Three months after everyone who knew had become depressed at the chances of a solution, it was solved by the Swedish-Canadian chemist Clarence Johnson, in charge of a Kellex laboratory in Jersey City. He did so by systematically going through all the possible solutions which combined what was good about previous versions.

His breakthrough caused a major rift among the senior engineers

---

[64] Groueff (2000), 176.
[65] Groueff (2000), 176.

connected with the Manhattan project – because, by January 1944, the plant that was to make the old inadequate membrane was nearly finished. Some of them, like Urey, didn't believe there would be enough time to switch production and they should concentrate on improving the old version. Others, like Keith from Kellex, wanted to go for broke on the Johnson version.

As always, it was down to Groves to listen to both sides and to make a decision. He decided to rip out all the equipment in the plant and to start all over again.

Chapter 10: Los Alamos

Unfortunately for Oppenheimer, life at Los Alamos was also far from simple. The baths for the whole community were in the old school buildings, but you could turn on the taps there or at home and worms would come out instead.

The original idea was that Los Alamos would be subsumed into the army. The heads of department would become majors, and so on. But people like Rabi and Szilard always resisted the idea of uniforms, so that idea was dropped. Teller arrived at almost the same time as Oppenheimer, to find that contractors had been on site throughout the freezing winter – but were told nothing about what they were building or why, which didn't make for good morale.

Oppie was formally appointed to run the laboratory on 25 February 1943. He spent some weeks discussing who should join them, and watching the emerging building of the horribly basic rows of homes for singles that were emerging there. It was soon clear that, if they wanted to persuade key scientists to live there, they would need to cater also for their wives and children.

It was a stressful period. In California, his old colleague Robert Wilson was sent to Los Alamos to prepare for the arrival of their cyclotron – and found chaos. He and physicist John Manley cornered Oppenheimer about this "and after a certain stage, Oppenheimer became extremely angry," he told Teller, and Oppenheimer's biographer, Paul Goodchild.[66] "He began to use vile language, asking us why we were telling him about these insignificant problems. That it was none of our business and so on. Both of us were scared to death."

Even so, resources weren't a problem. So, Los Alamos evolved quickly, until Oppenheimer had an organisational chart with 1,500 positions on it. Soon, there was also a town square, a cinema and

---

[66] Goodchild (2004), 77.

dance hall, plus a 19-piece dance band and a radio station.

**

Mici Teller arrived with baby Paul after the formal opening in April 1943. She had never warmed to Oppie and was sceptical about the whole project. She was soon leading the other women and wives to sit underneath the last few trees to protect them from the army contractors.

Oppenheimer had organised a series of introductory lectures once the official opening took place on 15 April.

Security was, as one might expect, extremely tight. Driving licences listed the addresses of everyone at Los Alamos as 'PO Box 1663'. Richard Feynman, a physicist from the theoretical division – and later a great populariser of science – used to enjoy playing practical jokes on the military security people. When he realised letters were being read and censored, he started sending letters to his wife and father with strange arrangements of dots and dashes. Then he explained that cryptography was just his hobby.

"Here we have assembled the greatest bunch of prima donnas ever seen in one place," Groves told military personnel at Los Alamos.[67]

It was amazing, given the conditions, that everyone managed to get on relatively well.

**

Mici hadn't wanted to bring a baby into the world, but as a result of his declaration of war on the USA, she was now convinced that Hitler would lose. Still, her husband left her with the baby and went to Los Alamos excited by the future.

He and Oppie shared a first-class compartment on the train from Chicago to Washington so that they could talk.

"We have a real job ahead," Oppenheimer was saying. "No

[67] Groueff (2000), 204.

matter what Groves demands now, we have to cooperate. But the time is coming when we will have to do things differently and resist the military."

Teller was shocked. "I don't think I would want to do that," he said. Oppenheimer changed the subject straight away and never raised it again. "I believe that the relationship between us changed at that instant," he wrote later.[68]

"Perhaps I over-reacted. Perhaps, if I had continued the conversation and probed for the point behind his remark, I might have obtained a better understanding, but Oppenheimer did not invite further questions or offer clarification, probing would have been discourteous, so I didn't ask."[69]

For Teller, the first great shock of the experience was when Oppenheimer gave the job of head of the theoretical division to Hans Bethe instead of him.

This had a disastrous effect on Teller's relationship with those around him. It was just too close for comfort to his childhood experience of constant rejection at school and university.

The British MAUD team had done most of the theoretical work, so he turned to thinking about his idea of a thermo-nuclear bomb, which he knew as the 'super'. The idea involved using a small nuclear explosion to ignite a 12kg slug of deuterium, which he believed would create as big a bang as a million tons of TNT – or about half the explosives used by both sides in World War II.

He was enraged that the S1 committee had decided that they must restrict their research to fission weapons while the war was still continuing.

"If your work was going to make any contribution to victory in World War II," wrote Bethe later, "it was essential that the whole laboratory agree on one or two major lines of development and that all else would be considered low priority."[70]

Oppenheimer was someone Teller considered himself close to –

---

[68] Goodchild (2004), 71.
[69] Goodchild (2004), 71-2.
[70] Goodchild (2004), 81.

yet he hadn't fought for the super with the governing board or appointed him to the job that best suited his talents. Instead, he had listened to people like Rabi slagging him off. For a sensitive man like Teller, this was intolerable.

In 1954, at Oppie's hearing a decade later, he was much more forgiving:

"I would like to say that I consider Dr Oppenheimer's direction of the Los Alamos laboratory as very outstanding, due mainly to the fact that with his very quick mind he found out very promptly what was going on in every part of the laboratory, made right judgements on things, supported work when it had to be supported – and I also think, with his very remarkable insight in psychological matters, made just a wonderful an executive director."[71]

The trouble was that Teller was saying these things during the trauma of the accusations against Oppenheimer in the 1950s, when some of their contemporaries felt he was speaking just a little too late. The truth was that Teller had never really recovered from Oppenheimer putting Berthe in charge of the theoretical division. And after that, Teller had refused to join in with anyone else's research work.

Yet Oppie knew how much he needed Teller and took the trouble to sit down with him every week after that, to listen to what he had been thinking.

**

By then, Oppenheimer clearly had something else on his mind. In the summer of 1943, he had a call from his old lover Jean Tatlock in California, where she was being treated for depression. He went there and spent a night and the following day with her, presumably aware that suspicious security officials would have a

---

[71] Bernstein (2004), 82-3.

field day watching him consort with a known communist.

Jean was to kill herself in the bath the following year.

Perhaps to offset the implications of this visit, in August, he dropped in to see the Berkeley security office to give them the name of someone they should be watching, a British engineer called George Eltenton, a communist and amateur spy, then living in California.

Lyall Johnson was the officer he spoke to. He reported the conversation to his boss, Colonel Boris Pash. In turn, Pash interviewed Oppenheimer, who told a long story about an intermediary – whose name he didn't pass on.

He faced tougher questioning by Groves' security advisor Colonel John Lansdale. He said he knew who it was, and they were blameless. You can order me to reveal it but, otherwise, I would like to keep it to myself, he told Lansdale.

In December 1943, Groves finally ordered him to name the person – it was his old communist friend Haakon Chevalier.

Grove took no further action, but Pash – who had secretly recorded his interview with Oppenheimer – felt that the wool was being pulled over his eyes. Oppie told him about the incident that summer when he was having dinner with the Chevaliers, and when they were alone in the kitchen – Chevalier had mentioned Eltenton to him.

But then Groves felt it was obvious that Oppenheimer was just sheltering his brother Frank, and he respected him for that. He also believed Oppie was essential to the all-important speed of the project. So, he protected him, despite the suspicions of the FBI, who were still following him everywhere and bugging his home and office.

**

Niels Bohr had always refused requests from the Danish underground to go to England to work on bombs – but his visit from Heisenberg had unnerved him. Another rough drawing was smuggled to him which implied that the Germans were making serious progress (they were: they got their first reactor running in

May 1942, six months before Fermi's effort on Stagg Field). But it was not for nearly two years, in September 1943, that the news reached Bohr and his brother Harald that the Nazis considered their family to be Jewish – their mother was Jewish – and that they were therefore in danger of arrest.

The Danish resistance helped Bohr and his wife escape by sea to Sweden at the end of the month and – the very next day – Bohr persuaded the Swedish king, Gustav V, to announce publicly Sweden's willingness to provide asylum to Jewish refugees. And so it was that, on 2 October 1943, Swedish radio broadcast that they were ready to offer asylum, and the mass rescue of the Danish Jews by their fellow Danes followed quickly afterwards. Over 7,000 Danish Jews escaped to Sweden.[72]

When the news of his escape reached the UK, Churchill's scientific advisor Lord Cherwell invited him over by telegram. Bohr arrived in Scotland on 6 October in a BOAC Mosquito aircraft, a high-speed bomber, converted to carry small, valuable cargoes or important passengers. They crossed German-occupied Norway by flying so high that they could avoid German fighters. Bohr, equipped with a parachute, flying suit and oxygen mask, spent the three-hour flight lying on a mattress in the aircraft's bomb bay. He passed out during the flight because he failed to hear the pilot's instruction to turn on his oxygen supply.

Bohr's son Aage followed his father to Britain on another flight a week later and became his personal assistant.

He arrived in the USA some weeks later, with Aage, and panicked Groves by showing him the German sketch. But the experts in Princeton decided, correctly, that this was not a diagram of a bomb – it was a reactor.

**

The US reactor design was still being developed by Fermi, and Wigner in Chicago. With the hyper-active Szilard as a gadfly who

---

[72] Pais (1992), 479.

couldn't keep still, going around the various laboratories offering advice.

Groves had put Du Pont in charge of building the first reactor. Yet there was no time to work out all the alternative solutions to the design problems that arose, and then test them. They had to put all their resources into developing the most likely looking candidate for a solution each time. Fermi would complain that "you're doing it all the wrong way".[73] They had to put up with that, aware that the scientists may have been brilliant, but they didn't really understand industrial processes.

That was Groves's hope – that Du Pont's engineers would solve the problems he asked them to – while he took the big decisions himself. As he did when he decided that the X-10 reactor at Oak Ridge would use a water-cooling system.

It was the same problem for Kellex, where Dobie Keith's teams were constructing a plant for gaseous diffusion, for purifying uranium-235. He was having major problems with his hydro pumps because, at the first test firing, every one of the pumps failed – because the seals all leaked.

The electromagnetic plant taking shape at Oak Ridge was also bogged down. The first track of the electromagnetic circuit (also codenamed Y-12) was fired up in December 1943, and it appeared to be working but, after a few days, there were increasing numbers of short circuits. Then finally it stopped.

Groves flew to Oak Ridge in a rage and ordered one of the new welded steel casings of the magnet to be broken open. And when it was, it was clear what the problem was – the cooling oil was carrying a sediment of rust and dirt, which had accumulated and shorted the whole plant.

They then had an added problem: the morale of the new workforce of thousands had sunk to its lowest point, enlivened only by an enthusiastic Lawrence who arrived quickly from Berkeley. At the same time, Tennessee Eastman staff raided the whole state for board games and movies, inspirational speakers

[73] Groueff (2000), 133.

and lecturers – anything to persuade the workforce not to get bored and wander away, while they fixed the cooling system.

Unfortunately, the plant carried on stopping, even after the magnets had been brought back and the pipes cleaned out.

It was a former chemistry professor, on the staff of Tennessee Eastman who came up with the idea that saved the day. He suggested that stainless steel would not be as good at releasing the precious uranium compared with copper, and that they should electroplate the insides of the magnets and the piping.

Lawrenec insisted that the job be done in one day – and it was.

**

The main point of contention at Los Alamos was now how to set off the bomb. Captain William 'Deke' Parsons – an experienced regular navy officer – was in charge of ballistics. And he favoured the 'gun method' – which meant that they would fire a small slug of uranium into another, larger sphere of uranium in the core. This method had been adopted from the start.

The only voice of disapproval came from Seth Neddermeyer – a young physicist from the National Standards Board – who proposed a different method at the introductory lectures. He wanted an *implosion* method to be used, whereby a hollow sphere of uranium, would be compressed inwards by a co-ordinated series of small explosions.

The issue was how to make sure the explosion was even all around – otherwise it would seep out and fail to work. Parsons was openly contemptuous of the whole idea.

But two things happened to rescue Neddermeyer's brainwave. First, was the arrival in Los Alamos of the great Hungarian-born mathematician and computing pioneer John von Neumann, who approved of implosion as a method and helped invent some lenses to concentrate the explosive waves, just as they would do with light waves.[74]

---

[74] Rhodes (1986), 575-8.

Then, came the discovery that a gun couldn't work with plutonium.

They had known from the outset that plutonium-240 might form spontaneously, alongside the isotope they wanted (plutonium-239) – they could not be separated. The danger was that, if there were other neutrons flying around – as there were, of course – then 240 was more likely to go for a little spontaneous fission, which might blow the core apart before it became critical. The latest calculations were that you would need a muzzle about 17 feet long. That would make for an unwieldy, uncomfortably massive bomb.

And – since it looked likely that they would only need 5kg of plutonium to reach a critical mass – and it was now being produced in some quantities at Hanford – it looked very much as though they would have to solve the implosion problem after all.

The British were now back involved again, following the Quebec agreement between Churchill and Roosevelt, so Groves took the opportunity to invite over Peierls and a group of 15 of them, led by Sir James Chadwick. – some of them went instead to Oak Ridge (Groves had asked them to review the gas diffusion mechanisms).

Plutonium had only been identified in practice in 1940 – Oppenheimer's former colleague from Caltech, the young chemist Glenn Seaborg. It became clear quite quickly that plutonium wouldn't have to be as pure as uranium-235 and was therefore easier to extract. The whole business caused a crisis for Oppenheimer. He even considered resignation, but he was persuaded to stay on by his friend Robert Bacher.

Oppenheimer and Groves then reorganised the laboratory. From then onwards, a small group worked on uranium. The rest worked on implosion – except for Teller, who once again refused.

"It appears sensible to discontinue the intensive effort to achieve higher purity for plutonium and to concentrate attention on methods of assembly which do not require a low neutron background for success," he wrote to Conant, about the design of the bomb that would eventually be known as 'Fat Man'. "At the present time, the method to which an overwhelming priority is assigned is the method of implosion."[75]

Parsons was furious at the new division of responsibilities. Luckily for Oppenheimer, he still had a great deal to be getting along with, designing the gun trigger for the uranium bomb. Teller and Von Neumann between them came up with a solution to the complex design of the plutonium version. Oppenheimer agreed that they should start looking at this solution straight away, and shifted the direction of research within a week.

Teller was still trying to get back to the super, but the S1 committee re-evaluated it in November 1943, not aware that plutonium was much easier to ignite than uranium-235. The fuel would also need some tritium and, above all, it would take far too long – or so they said.

Bethe asked Teller to take on the calculations for the implosion. He said no – which marked the end of what had been a long friendship between the two men.

"Not only were other people more capable than I of providing such work," wrote Teller later, "but I also suspected that a job that formidable might not be completed in time to have any influence on a bomb that could be used during the war."

In the event, Oppenheimer asked if Rudolf Peierls could help. He was in Los Alamos by that time, with the 'Tube Alloys' (the British code word for their atomic bomb project) mission to the USA.

Teller had gotten into the habit of getting up late and staying up late, playing the piano. To his closest colleagues, he seemed increasingly thin-skinned. When Oppenheimer held a party, some months after this, and he forgot to ask Peierls, he went straight round to Peierls' office the next day to apologise. "But there is an element of relief in this situation," Oppenheimer confided. "It might have happened with Edward Teller!"

At this time, Teller was reading *Darkness at Noon*, Arthur Koestler's classic novel about tyranny, and thinking about his old colleagues who had been arrested during Stalin's purges –

---

[75] Rhodes (1986), 548.

especially the purge in Ukraine.

Groves was also deeply suspicious of Soviet Russia. It was a lonely time to have that opinion, when everyone else seemed to be cheering them on.

Among these was Klaus Fuchs, who – as well as being part of the same Tube Alloys mission – was an anti-Nazi, the son of a Lutheran pastor. He had been interned in the UK at the outbreak of war, then rescued by Peierls – one of Peierls's conditions of coming to the USA was that he should bring Fuchs with him.

All the allies knew at this stage of the war was that the Nazis were building concrete bunkers across northern Europe, for Hitler's new 'super weapons.' Scientists connected with the Manhattan project feared that they were for launching nuclear rockets. Colonel Pash was sent into Europe in the autumn of 1944 to find out how far they had got. In November 1944, when Strasbourg fell, he dashed in and seized von Weiszaker's laboratory there – and it was clear that the Nazis had failed to make much progress since 1942. They seemed to him to be uncertain that a chain reaction was even possible.

It was beginning to look as though it was going to be alright. By the end of 1944, two reactors at the Hanford site were up and running, despite setbacks – like when they discovered that xenon absorbed deuterons at an extraordinary rate. Groves was finally optimistic, and he told General George Marshall, his boss as chief of staff to the army, that he expected to have 18 5kg bombs by the second half of 1945 – six months ahead.

"It looks like a race," Conant confided to his diary, "to see whether a fat man or a thin man will be dropped first, and whether the month will be July, August or September."[76]

---

[76] Rhodes (1986), 560.

Chapter 11: The Trinity test

Early in 1945, designs for the bomb were well-advanced – two of them, in fact: there was enough uranium-235 only for one bomb ('Little Boy'), and the bomb they would have to test would be an 'implosion bomb', codenamed 'Fat Man'. The test was scheduled for mid-July.

The military committee had decided that they would use it on Japan instead of Germany – but nobody told them at Los Alamos for months.

Szilard and Einstein were lobbying to make sure that this didn't happen – certainly with no warning. Szilard was organising a petition.

"I personally feel that it could be a matter of importance if a large number of scientists who would have worked in this field went clearly and unmistakably on the record as to their opposition on moral grounds to the use of these bombs in the present phase of the war," he wrote in a letter circulated to scientists he knew.[77] One letter arrived at Los Alamos with Teller, who sympathised – but wanted to talk to Oppenheimer before he signed.

Then suddenly, at the height of all this speculation and debate, on 12 April 1945, Roosevelt died. His vice-president, Harry Truman, knew nothing about the Bomb, though as a prominent senator, he had been trying to find out where these untold millions were disappearing to.

Together, Groves and Henry Stimson briefed him. They proposed an interim committee to decide how it should be used. Oppenheimer was drafted in as chair of the scientific panel – and he involved Fermi, Compton and Lawrence.

General George Marshall and Oppenheimer suggested they might approach the Russians with a view to co-operation. This was immediately vetoed by Truman's Secretary of State James Byrnes.

---

[77] Goodchild (2004), 100.

In ten minutes over lunch, committee members also discussed whether to issue a warning. They decided that, if they did so, they might face human shields.

Meanwhile, in Chicago, Szilard had the university in an uproar. James Franck wrote a paper as a result which warned that an unannounced attack on Japan would "precipitate the race for armaments".[78]

Teller went to see Oppenheimer about the petition, and he was defensive. "What do they know about Japanese psychology?" he asked Teller. "How can they judge the way to end the war?"[79]

"I did not circulate Szilard's petition," Teller wrote later. "Today, I regret that I did not."[80]

It is odd, given what he was to become, that Teller was at all swayed by Szilard's petition – but there was an edge of desperation about his reply to Szilard:

"I should like to have the advice of all of you whether it is a crime to continue to work, but I feel I should do the wrong thing if I tried to say how to tie the little toe of the ghost to the bottle from which we just helped it to escape."[81]

Is it that his opinions were not yet settled, or that he was feeling the isolation as his views and those of so many scientists began to diverge – when they had dropped everything to make sure Hitler was not the first one to develop a bomb.

Churchill at the Potsdam conference was among those clear on either side that the use of the first bomb was obvious:

"There never was a moment's discussion as to whether the bomb should be used or not," he wrote later. "The historic fact remains

---

[78] Goodchild (2004), 102.
[79] *Ibid.*
[80] *Ibid.*, Also in Edward Teller (2001), *Memoirs: A 20th century journey in science and politics.* New York: Perseus Press, 206f.
[81] Goodchild (2004), 103.

… that the decision whether or not to use the atomic bomb to compel the Japanese to surrender was never an issue … there was universal, automatic, unquestioned agreement around our table; … I never heard the slightest suggestion that we should do otherwise."

No declaration or ultimatum was issued in the final warning to Japan under the names of Truman, Chiang Kai-Shek and Clement Attlee – the result of the UK general election came half-way through the Potsdam conference and Churchill was out of office. Stalin was not yet at war with Japan. There was no mention of a new weapon with extraordinary destructive power.

**

The Fat Man implosion bomb had such a revolutionary design that it simply had to be tested. The test was set for 12 July and Oppenheimer called it 'Trinity' – it is said this was a tribute to Jean Tatlock, because the poem "batter, my heart, three-personed God", by John Donne, was among her favourites.

Weather forecasts delayed the test until 16 July. The Harvard experimental physicist Kenneth Bainbridge – and his staff of 25 – had been asked to take charge of the test, and he had chosen the 18-by-24 mile site on the Alamogordo Bombing Range back in May 1944.

Fermi arrived as a consultant. The British metallurgist Cyril Smith took the two half spheres of plutonium from the vault – only to find that the nickel casing, to absorb alpha particles, was beginning to blister – which meant they wouldn't fit exactly. Smith's teams solved the problem by grinding the blisters partly off and smoothing the sides with sheets of gold foil.[82]

It was more than 200 miles from Los Alamos to the test site. Drivers were given strict instructions that, when they got south of Albuquerque, they should avoid any contact with anyone. If

---

[82] Rhodes (1985), 657-8.

anyone asked them, they should say they worked for 'Engineer of Albuquerque'.

There was still only enough uranium for one Little Boy bomb, which could use the gun method organised by Parsons' team. Two Los Alamos scientists, dressed as army artillery officers to avoid too much attention, had already been flown to San Francisco with the pieces of the bomb.

At dawn on the day of the test, they all went on board the cruiser *Indianapolis,* bound for Tinian Island in the western Pacific. The captain was told nothing about his cargo except that, if the ship sank, then the cylinder – which was welded to the floor of the scientists' cabin – was to have priority over sailors for rescue.

Meanwhile, July 16 was in the middle of the Potsdam conference of the allied leaders. Truman, Attlee and Churchill were still expecting a message about how the test had gone, because it would govern their policy towards Stalin.

Fermi was in Los Alamos as a consultant, worrying about whether the explosion would ignite the air. Calculations had always suggested it wouldn't – but could you ever be quite sure? Oppenheimer was going through the possibilities with his scientists.

Teller had arrived at the site the day before. The weather was terrible and it was steadily getting worse. Fermi was afraid a sudden gust of wind would deluge the test site with radioactive fall-out. Oppenheimer was worrying that the wind might set off the bomb prematurely or might knock it off its hundred-foot metal mast.

Groves took Oppenheimer down into the control bunker, talking intensely about the future. They agreed to decide whether to go ahead at 1 am, but the wind and rain was getting worse.

Groves was feeling protective towards Oppenheimer, who was looking ashen-faced with worry, and cross with Fermi who was taking bets with anyone who was around him about whether the bomb would set light to the atmosphere and destroy New Mexico or the whole world.

Between decisions, Groves was sleeping in a tent with Conant and Bush, who had also just arrived.

At 2 am, the weather began to improve, and the meteorologist assured Groves that it would improve at dawn.

"You'd better be right on this," he said to the meteorologist. "Or I'll hang you!"[83]

Groves decided the test would take place at 5.30 am., then he stumped off to get the governor of New Mexico out of bed to tell him that he might have to declare martial law.

At 4 in the morning of 16 July, the rain stopped.

The countdown began at 5.10 am. At base camp, five miles from the zero point, where Conant, Bush and Groves were, they were told to lie on the ground face down, with their hands over their eyes.

On Compania Hill, 30 miles away, Teller had brought sun tan lotion and with five minutes to go, he was slathering on his face, and offering it around. He didn't want to turn his back, so he took some welders' glasses and put on dark glasses underneath them, plus gloves to press the glasses onto his face.

The countdown stopped with five seconds to go. "During those last five seconds, we all lay there, quietly, waiting for what seemed an eternity, wondering whether the bomb had failed or had been delayed once again," wrote Teller:[84]

"Then I saw a faint point of light that appeared to divide into three horizontal points... As the question 'Is this all?' flashed through my mind, I remembered my extra protection. As the luminous points faded, I lifted my right hand to admit a little light under the welder's glasses. It was as if I had pulled open the curtain on a dark night."

The scientists stood now, watching fascinated. Then there was a loud crack across the 30 miles as the sound wave hit them from across the desert.

At base camp, 10,000 yards south of the explosion,

---

[83] Rhodes (1986), 666.
[84] Goodchild (2004), 105.

Oppenheimer had been propping himself up against a post, chain smoking and looking drawn and worried. Although he had turned away from the flash, they were suddenly aware of the dazzling light, pouring in from the back door of their bunker.

"A few people laughed, a few people cried, most people were silent," wrote Oppenheimer later.[85] "There flashed through my mind a line from the *Bhagavadghita* in which Krishna is trying to persuade the prince that he should do his duty: 'I am become death, the destroyer of worlds."

William Laurence of the *New York Times* – the only media representative invited – wrote that "it was like the grand finale of a mighty symphony of the elements".[86]

Groves called his secretary from Albuquerque, and she passed it onto Stimson, now in Potsdam: "Operation done this morning. Diagnosis is not yet completed but results seem satisfactory and are already exceeding expectations ... Dr Groves pleased..."[87]

Alamogordo Air Base issued a press release later that same day:

"The Commanding Officer of the Alamogordo Air Base made the following statement today:

Several inquiries have been received concerning a heavy explosion which occurred on the Alamogordo Air Base reservation this morning.

A remotely located ammunition magazine containing a considerable amount of high explosives and pyrotechnics exploded.

There was no loss of life and the property damage outside the explosive magazine itself was negligible.

Weather conditions affecting the content of gas shells exploded

---

[85] Goodchild (2004), 198. From Lee Gianoveti and Fred Freed (1985), *The Decision to drop the bomb.* New York: Coward-McCann, 189.

[86] Groueff (2000), 355.

[87] James W. Kunetka (1982), *Oppenheimer: The years of risk.* Englewood Cliffs, New Jersey: Prentice-Hall, 72.

by the blast may make it desirable for the Army to evacuate temporarily a few civilians from their homes."[88]

**

Five days later, on 21 July, Groves' full report arrived with Truman at the Potsdam conference. It was a huge relief to the allied leaders. They no longer needed Russian help to finish the war in Japan, which meant they could check Soviet ambitions in the Far East. Truman decided to tell Stalin about it. And so, on 24 July, he casually mentioned that they had "a new weapon of unusual destructive force".

To his great surprise, Stalin seemed completely familiar with the idea. He said he was glad to hear it and that he hoped they would make "good use of it against the Japanese".[89]

By then Fuchs had filled in most of the gaps in his knowledge, and brilliant Russian scientists like Andrei Sacharov were ready at their laboratories.

"That was carrying casualness rather far," said Oppenheimer, with studied understatement.[90]

---

[88] Groueff (2000), 357.
[89] Rhodes (1986), 690.
[90] *Ibid.*

Chapter 12: Dropping a bomb and the aftermath

The world knows that the bomb known as 'Little Boy' was taken in pieces by the cruiser *Indianapolis* to Tinian Island, about six hours flying time from Tokyo. They don't know that the original target had been Kyoto, but this had been vetoed by the 77-year-old Secretary for War, Henry Stimson – he had been there for his honeymoon, decades before and he didn't like the bombing of cities anyway

"The reputation of the United States for fair play and humanitarianism is the world's biggest asset for peace in the coming decades," he told Truman in May.[91]

On 6 August 1945, having been loaded on board the B-29 Superfortress *Enola Gay,* Captain Paul Tibbets leaned out of the pilot's seat to give watchers a cheery wave – Groves had insisted the the whole business should be filmed for posterity, so the runway was floodlit. Two other B-29s also climbed into the air.

All three made their way separately to Iwo Jima, when they set a joint course for Japan. By the time they had reached 32,000 feet over Hiroshima, it was clear visibility. The crew had armed the bomb during the flight to minimise the risks during take-off. And the safety devices had been removed 30 minutes before. They opened the bomb doors and let the first nuclear bomb to be used in anger go at exactly 8.15 in the morning local time.

Everything went as planned, and Little Boy took 73 seconds to fall to its predetermined detonation height – at just less than 2,000 feet, or 600 metres. above the city. *Enola Gay* turned away quickly and managed to go about 11.5 miles before the crew felt the shock waves from the blast.

The explosion was a blast equivalent to 16 kilotons of TNT (the Trinity test had measured about 18). It completely flattened an area of about one mile in radius. Fire and destruction spread out for

---

[91] Rhodes (1986), 639-630.

another about 4.4 square miles.[92] Japanese officials said later that the bomb had demolished about 69 per cent of buildings and damaged up to another 7 per cent.

It also killed about 70,000 to 80,000 people, or about 30 percent of the city's population, either in the explosion or the resultant firestorm, with another 70,000 injured.[93] Out of those killed, 20,000 were soldiers and 20,000 were Korean slave labourers.

The first American journalist to interview some of the survivors in Hiroshima was John Hersey, whose book *Hiroshima* has been in print ever since. It was commissioned and published in a whole issue of the *New Yorker* magazine. In it, he told the story of six survivors.

Like Toshiko Sasaki, who was at her desk in the personnel department of a tin factory. At exactly 8.15am, she was talking to a fellow employee when the room filled with "a blinding light".[94] The flash was so powerful that it pushed over a bookshelf, crushing her leg and leaving her hidden underneath it while the building collapsed around her.

After going home from a safe area, Mrs Hatsuyo Nakamura, a widow with three children – her husband had been killed fighting in Singapore – saw a flash "whiter than any white she had" seen before. She was thrown into the next room while her three children were buried in debris.

Standing alone in a corridor of his hospital, Dr Terufumi Sasaki (no relation to Toshiko) saw a "gigantic photographic flash". The explosion tore the hospital apart but Dr Sasaki remained

---

[92] US Government (1946), *'Radiation Dose Reconstruction US Occupation Forces in Hiroshima and Nagasaki, Japan, 1945-1946' (DNA 5512F)*
[93] https://www.trumanlibrary.gov/whistlestop/study_collections/bomb/large/documents/index.php?pagenumber=42&documentid=65&documentdate=1946-0619&studycollectionid=abomb
[94] John Hersey (1946), 'Hiroshima', *New Yorker*, 22 Aug. Available at
https://www.newyorker.com/magazine/1946/08/31/hiroshima

miraculously untouched, except his glasses and shoes had been blown off his body. Next, he found he was the only doctor to be unhurt in the hospital, as it quickly began to fill with patients.

Mrs Nakamura travelled with her children and neighbour to Asano Park at the Jesuit mission house. The whole family was vomiting continuously.

As patients filled every inch of what remained of the hospital, Dr Sasaki became like a robot, repeating the same treatments on patient after patient.

Meanwhile, Toshiko Sasaki was still lying unconscious under the bookshelf and crumbled building. Her leg was severely broken. She was propped up alongside two badly wounded people and abandoned.

Chapter 3 chronicled the days after the dropping of the bomb, the continuing troubles faced by the survivors, and the possible explanations for the massive devastation that the witnesses had ever seen.

On August 12, the Nakamuras were still being sick and they found that the rest of their family had all died. By then, 10,000 had shown up at the Red Cross Hospital. Dr Sasaki was still trying to attend to as many people as possible – but all that could be done is to put saline on the worst burns. Dead patients were lying everywhere. Poor Toshiko Sasaki was still left with no help outside the factory until, finally, friends came to find her body and she was transferred to a hospital.

By August 15, the war was over. Mrs Nakamura still felt sick and her hair began to fall out. Once given the okay that the radiation levels in Hiroshima were acceptable and her appearance was presentable, she returned to her home to retrieve her sewing machine but it was rusted and ruined.

Toshiko Sasaki was still in hospital and in pain. The infection had prevented doctors from being able to set her fractured leg. She was discharged at the end of April 1946, severely crippled. Dr Sasaki had been studying the progression of patients and assigned three stages to the disease. After six months, the Red Cross Hospital began to function normally. A year after the bomb, Toshiko Sasaki was disabled, Mrs Nakamura was destitute, and Dr

Sasaki was not capable of the work he had once done.

These were not the dead. Hersey also described people with melted eyeballs, or people vaporised, leaving only their shadows etched onto walls.[95] And all those children who abandoned their mothers in the initial panic, only to go back and find them dead.

It made for a tough read. One of the Los Alamos scientists was reported to have been reduced to tears by it.[96]

**

Three days after the horror of Hiroshima, the second bomb – Fat Boy, designed also to test the implosion device – followed on Nagasaki. The original plan had been scheduled for 11 August, but it was brought forward by two days to 9 August because of bad weather forecasts.

It was also planned to attack Kokura. This time, the bomb was carried by B-29 *Bockscar*, flown by Major Charles Sweeney. *Enola Gay* reported clear skies over Kokura, but by the time *Bockscar* arrived, the city was obscured by smoke from fires from the conventional bombing of Yahata by 224 B-29s the day before. After three unsuccessful passes, *Bockscar* diverted to its secondary target, Nagasaki, where it dropped its bomb.

In contrast to the Hiroshima mission, the Nagasaki mission has been described as tactically botched, although the mission did meet its objectives. The crew had very little fuel by the time they landed at the emergency backup landing site on Okinawa. One engine gave out as they came in to land.

There have been various estimates of the immediate death toll of between 40,000 and 70,000. The bomb landed near the Mitsubishi works there, which was completely obliterated, but the power was directed by the hills mainly down a valley away from the main part

---

[95] Hersey, John (1973). *Hiroshima*. New York: Alfred. Knopf, 69 & 96.
[96] Gerard J. DeGroot (2005), *The Bomb: A life*. Cambridge, Mass.: Harvard Press.

of the city.

After Nagasaki, Truman ordered a halt to the bombing – assuming that the Japanese would surrender – before his deadline of August 15, when the Russians had said they would declare war.

The military junta in charge of Japan had still not agreed, so the Emperor Hirohito forced the issue. They offered to surrender, this time via Switzerland not Moscow, with the single proviso that "it does not compromise any demand which prejudices the prerogatives of His Majesty as a sovereign ruler."

This offer arrived in Washington the morning after Nagasaki had been bombed. Stimson prevailed upon Truman, and they sent a deliberately compromised and ambiguous message to the Japanese, proposed by James Forrestal, the Secretary of the Navy, that communicated their "willingness to accept, yet define the terms of surrender in such a manner that the intent and purposes of the Potsdam Declaration would be clearly accomplished."[97]

And so it was that the end of the war with Japan came about on virtually the same terms that had been offered, via Moscow, before the bombing.

**

A feeling of depression covered the laboratories at Los Alamos after the news arrived of the attacks.

Truman had been thrilled when he heard about the bombing of Hiroshima on his way home from Potsdam. Groves had phoned Oppenheimer in the afternoon of August 6.

"Yes, it has been a long road and I think one of the wisest things I ever did was when I selected the director of Los Alamos," he said.

"Well, I have my doubts, General Groves," said Oppenheimer.

"Well, you know I've never concurred with those doubts at any time."[98]

---

[97] Rhodes (1986), 735.
[98] Rhodes (1986), 742.

But as the news of the damage began to emerge, the Los Alamos scientists began to feel their own doubts about what they had enabled. And even more so when – a month later – a scientist sent to take a look at the wreckage reported back that "we circled finally low over Hiroshima and stared in disbelief. There below us was flat level ground of what had been a city, scorched red," said Phil Morrison.[99]

"Using atomic bombs against Japan is one of the greatest blunders in history," wrote Szilard.[100]

"At first I refused to believe that this could be true, but in the end, I had to face the fact that it was officially confirmed by the president of the United States," wrote Otto Hahn, interned in the English countryside with other German nuclear scientists.[101] "I was shocked and depressed beyond measure. The thought of the unspeakable misery of countless innocent women and children was something that I could scarcely bear."

Oppenheimer now desperately wanted to get away from nuclear research and to go back to academia. He resolved to go in October 1945, when he was handing over the laboratory to the army, in the person of General Groves.

His farewell speech pre-figured much of the debate that was to follow for the rest of his life:

"If atomic bombs are to be added to the arsenals of a warring world, or the arsenals of nations preparing for war, then the time will come when, mankind will curse the names of Los Alamos and Hiroshima; the peoples of this world must unite or they will perish. This war that has ravaged so much of the earth, has written these words. The atomic bomb has spelled them out for all men to understand."[102]

---

[99] Goodchild (2004), 169.
[100] Rhodes (1986), *op. cit.*
[101] *Ibid.*
[102] Goodchild (1980), 173.

Chapter 13: Fallout

Exactly why Strauss had turned down his promotion to rear-admiral in 1944 was never quite clear. Was it, as he suggested, because it would have interfered with his campaign on behalf of naval reserve officers everywhere. Or was it because Roosevelt couldn't stand him?

Either way, the death of the president cleared away one hurdle. Truman had no idea who he was.

Admiral Ernest King was the butt of an unfortunate joke by Strauss which he overheard after Pearl Harbor. They met again in 1946 when King invited him "very graciously" to lunch, and told him he had misjudged him. Strauss then risked another of his jokes, when he said he had used to claim that King was the equivalent of two Japanese task forces. "To my immense relief, he laughed," wrote Strauss. "We remained good friends for the rest of his life."[103]

By then, he had got his promotion to rear-admiral after all. He also persuaded the navy secretary James Forrestal to launch an office of research and inventions, before the end of the war. It later became the Office of Naval Research.

When later in the war, he had been running Forrestal's office, he was sent a young lieutenant-commander called Douglas Fairbanks Jr. This caused chaos in the office because the girls working there got so over-excited that Fairbanks was transferred to sea – which was just what he wanted. By 1944, Strauss was chairing the navy's munitions board. His influence, and his basic charm, were growing considerably.

Early in 1946, he went to see Forrestal again, for lunch. Forrestal's emaciated appearance demonstrated how hard he had taken Truman's request that he resign in favour of Colonel Louis Johnson. Strauss said that it was shattering to hear his old boss

---

[103] Strauss (1963), 143.

describing himself as a failure. And he tried to reassure him – that he had succeeded more than anyone in the same job.[104]

Sadly, Forrestal killed himself in the early hours of 23 May 1946. "By the time he was plumbing the depths of despair from a kind of depression with which many physicians had become familiar during the war, a condition associated with severe and prolonged emotional fatigue."[105]

**

Teller was back in Chicago after the war, frustrated that his former colleagues were still ignoring the potential of the 'super'. He was also feeling peculiarly jealous of the acknowledged 'father of the Bomb', Oppenheimer.

Oppenheimer himself was feeling torn between his responsibility for the nuclear world and his need to escape everything and go back into academic theory at CalTech.

He confided this to Truman, the first time he met him. It didn't go well. He was 41 and far too thin, after his exertions at Los Alamos. He was "hesitant and cheerless", according to Dean Acheson, Truman's Secretary of State, who was there. Truman asked what the matter was.

"I feel we have blood on our hands," he said.

"Never mind," said Truman. "It will all come out in the wash. When will the Russians be able to build a bomb?"

"I don't know," said Oppie.

"Never," said Truman, answering his own question.

When Oppenheimer had gone, Truman told Acheson: "After all, all he did was make the bomb – I'm the guy who fired it off! Don't bring him here again."[106]

There then followed months of wrangling over whether the military or civilians would control the new weapons and the

---

[104] Strauss (1963), 181.

[105] Strauss (1963), 161.

[106] Bernstein (2004), 102.

Atomic Energy Act, passed unanimously by the senate, set up an Atomic Energy Commission (AEC). It was chaired by the former chair of the Tennessee Valley Authority, David Lilienthal, a lifelong admirer of Oppenheimer – who was not picked as a commissioner himself, but he was drafted in to chair the GAC, their General Advisory Committee.

What should happen next? The Acheson-Lilienthal Report attempted to answer the question. It had been drafted by Oppenheimer and reworked by Lilienthal, until it was 34,000 words long. In March 46, they spent four days discussing the draft at Dumbarton Oaks in Washington.

Acheson looked up from reading it and said: "This is a brilliant and profound document."[107]

The plan was to organise an international atomic development authority to take ownership of all uranium mines, and all nuclear material and nuclear research laboratories.

Unfortunately, Truman was persuaded to choose the elderly Wall Street financier Bernard Baruch to put forward the plan at the United Nations general assembly.

The trouble was that Soviet policy was even more rigid than the Americans. Yes, it was going to be a tough sell to the Russians, but the position "should be to make an honourable proposal and thus find out if they have the will to cooperate," said Oppenheimer.[108]

Baruch and his friends were investors in Newmont Mining Corporation, and would have lost millions if their uranium mines had been given away to the UN. He also emphasised the punitive stuff – what would happen if anyone broke the agreement. So, it was hardly a surprise that the Russians dismissed Baruch's

---

[107] Joseph Lieberman (1970), *The Scorpion and the Tarantula: The struggle to control atomic weapons*, New York: Houghton Mifflin, 255. Quoted in Kai Bird and Martin J. Sherwin (2008*), American Prometheus: The triumph and taregdy of J. Robert Oppenheimer.* London: Atlantic Books, 341.

[108] Bird & Sherwin (2008), 343.

proposal out of hand, on the grounds that it would maintain the American monopoly of atomic weapons indefinitely.

When he heard about Oppenheimer's involvement with the Acheson-Lilienthal plan, J. Edgar Hoover at the FBI gave the order to have Oppenheimer tailed and authorised wire taps at his home. The decision was based on no evidence at all. Worse, he was now seriously depressed. "And I find that physics and the teaching of physics, which is my life, now seems irrelevant," he told Lilienthal.[109]

**

In July 1946, the fourth bomb blast took place in Bikini Atoll. Oppenheimer didn't go to this test – partly because it had been timed to coincide with Baruch's presentation to the UN. Instead, he wrote a long letter to Truman eviscerating the idea of tests on whether nuclear weapons could sink battleships – the main purpose of the Bikini tests – of course they could: it could have all been worked out mathematically.[110]

Strauss had meanwhile been trying to get the government to set up listening stations – long-range detection equipment, capable of recording any nuclear test the Russians had planned. At that stage in the Cold War, the earliest anyone in the USA believed they could test a bomb was 1952.

It was a uniquely dangerous moment for the world. The British philosopher Bertrand Russell – who was later to be a major campaigner for nuclear disarmament – was even advocating threatening a pre-emptive strike on the Russians, as the only way to avoid the possibility of a nuclear-armed world war – because nobody would survive that.[111]

---

[109] *Ibid.*

[110] Bird & Sherwin (2008), 348-9.

[111] David Blitz (2002), *Did Russell Advocate Preventive Atomic War Against the USSR?* David Blitz, New Britain, CT. https://www.google.co.uk/search?q=russell+cnd+prre-

OPPENHEIMER: A WORLD DESTROYED

Early in July 1947, the FBI leaked the news to the *Washington Times-Despatch* that Oppie's brother Frank Oppenheimer had been a communist. 'US Atom Scientist's Brother Exposed as a Communist Who Worked on A-Bomb', said the resulting headline.

**

The difficulties between Oppenheimer and Strauss began 18 months later, in February 1949. They knew each other because, in 1947, the Institute for Advanced Study in Princeton was looking for a new director to succeed Einstein. As a trustee, Strauss – who had been in the running as a candidate himself – had been deputed to offer the job to Oppenheimer. He accepted.

Then, when it was clear that employees at the Argonne lab had discovered 289g of uranium was missing, it had taken them six weeks to own up to the officials in Washington, some hard-liners called for Lilienthal to be sacked.

Then there was a congressional hearing about this and other security matters, which Lilienthal welcomed as a chance to redeem their reputation.

Strauss himself gave evidence for two days in June, explaining why he had always opposed sending radioactive isotopes abroad – in case they found their way into unfriendly hands and endangered national security.

But Oppenheimer knew that isotopes could not be used for

---

emoptive+strike&tbm=isch&ved=2ahUKEwjazO7i87v9AhUBs
UwKHXBqA24Q2-cCegQIABAA&oq=russell+cnd+prre-
emoptive+strike&gs_lcp=CgNpbWcQAzoECCMQJzoFCAAQg
AQ6BggAEAcQHjoECAAQHjoJCAAQgAQQChAYOggIABC
xAxCDAToICAAQgAQQsQM6CwgAEIAEELEDEIMBOgYIA
BAFEB5Q5htYzWRgym1oAHAAeACAAY8HiAGzGJIBCDM
wLjIuNi0xmAEAoAEBqgELZ3dzLXdpei1pbWfAAQE&sclient
=img&ei=ZuL_Y9qBK4HisgLw1I3wBg&authuser=0&bih=569
&biw=1263&hl=en#imgrc=Gbg6COxdT_2BEM

79

fission, and he made the mistake of making fun of him. "No man can force me to say that you cannot use these isotopes for atomic energy," said Oppenheimer. "You can use a shovel for atomic energy – in fact, you do. You can use a bottle of beer for atomic energy – in fact, you do. But to get some perspective, the fact is that, during the war and after the war, these materials have played no significant part, and in my knowledge no part at all... My own rating of the importance of isotopes in the broad sense is that they are far less important [for national defence] than electronic devices, but far more important than, let us say, vitamins. Somewhere in between."[112]

Most of the audience laughed but Strauss didn't. Oppenheimer's friend, AEC counsel Joe Volpe, saw the look on Strauss's face as he stormed out – his eyes narrowed and his face flushed – and he realised his friend had made an enemy.

"How did I do?" Oppenheimer asked him.

"Too well, Robert – much too well."[113]

Strauss always wanted to be a physicist and he couldn't stand anyone disrespecting his knowledge.

[112] Kunetka (1982), 144.
[113] Bernstein (2004), 109.

Chapter 14: The super

Strauss had insisted that the government should equip and send up planes especially fitted with equipment to detect atomic blasts. On 3 September 1949, one of these over the Pacific picked up signs of an explosion. It took two weeks for the air force to send as many planes as they could to collect air samples over the Pacific – but it was clear that the Soviets had probably carried out a nuclear test.

Lilienthal dashed back from holiday in Martha's Vineyard. He and Oppenheimer were urging Truman to go public on the discovery. "We mustn't muff this chance to end the miasma of secrecy … holding a secret where there is no secret."[114]

Truman, who was particularly shocked at the news – having convinced himself that the 'Asiatics' could never build a bomb – eventually announced it at the end of the month. There happened to be a huge thunderclap over Washington as he did so, which added to the sense of impending peril.

The big question among those few who knew and understood these issues was how America should respond – and specifically, what to do about Teller's super.

Strauss – now an AEC commissioner – wanted a Manhattan Project-style national effort to make it real. Lilienthal, Acheson and Oppenheimer agreed that a major danger was that it might come to dominate foreign policy – but what was the alternative? Especially now that the Soviets were snapping at their heels.

**

Early in 1948, the world had witnessed the Berlin airlift, the invasion of Czechoslovakia by the Soviets and – at the same time

---

[114] Kunetka (1982) 147. From David Lilienthal (1964), *the Journals of David E. Lilienthal, Vol II,1945-1950.* New York: Harper & Row, 572.

– Americans believed themselves to be suffering from a serious shortage of nuclear weapons.

Even so, the Eniwetok Atoll test in the Spring of 1948 was considered a great success, when they exploded a redesigned fission bomb, three or four times the size of the Nagasaki bomb using only half the plutonium.

Now they could also use the same basic technology to make much smaller bombs, for use on battlefields, as well as bigger ones, up to 40 or 50 times bigger than Nagasaki.

Because of the increased pressure on him to deliver, Los Alamos director Norris Brdadbury asked Teller if he would go back there. He did, though he kept his connection with Chicago. He also went to see Heisenberg, who he found isolated in East Germany. Going back to Los Alamos meant also going back to his frustrating partnership with the Polish mathematician Stan Ulam, who he didn't get on with.

Oppenheimer was especially worried about the emerging hysteria about the bomb that was emerging in Washington. If the Russians could catch up so fast, may be that they really could be first to the super. That was the story Teller was putting across to anyone who would listen.

Truman didn't believe it – nobody except for Teller thought they would manage to produce a Soviet H-bomb for a decade. But he also had Strauss on his side.

At this stage, most of the designs for the 'super' were vast. One had a diameter of 162 feet. Lilienthal was trying to avoid discussion about the super. He tried to block discussion of a paper by Strauss which called for a "quantum jump" in efforts towards the super. But Strauss circulated it anyway – then he went to see Admiral Souers, a member of the National Security Council and close to Truman.

His hunch paid off. Not only had Souers never heard about the super, but neither had Truman. The president told Souers to "tell Strauss to go to it".[115]

---

[115] Goodchild (2004), 144.

The same day, Luis Alvarez called Teller from Berkeley. He and Lawrence were on their way to Los Alamos, because they were afraid that the Russians had made more progress on the super than the Americans had.

Teller also began sending memos about how the Russians were probably using heavy water, which would have made it easier for them to produce tritium – a key component of the H-bomb. Alvarez and Lawrence spent some days in Washington, pressing people about the urgency. Lilienthal was short and cold with them – but that cut no ice with the politicians and military types who were increasingly convinced that the future lay with Teller's super. Not many knew, as Oppenheimer did, that the USA already had a stockpile of 169 warheads.

Teller then went to see Bethe and Fermi to persuade them to come back to Los Alamos. Fermi said no, but Bethe said he would. Then he changed his mind when he went to see Oppenheimer in Princeton.

Bethe had also taken the opportunity to go to a university meeting, organised by the Emergency Committee of Atomic Scientists, run by Einstein and Szilard. But when he heard two days later, Teller blamed the mysterious hypnotic power of Oppie that persuaded Bethe that, as his wife said, "there was enough bang already".[116]

Oppenheimer was, in fact, very careful with what he was saying about the H-bomb – though he had shown Bethe the letter he had received from Conant, saying that it would be built "over my dead body".[117]

But in reply to Conant, he expressed what he really thought: "I am not sure that the miserable thing will work," he wrote. "Nor that it can be gotten to a target except by ox cart... What does worry me is that this thing appears to have caught the imaginations of both the congressional and military people, as the answer to the problem posed by the Russian advance... We have always known

---

[116] Goodchild (2004), 146-7.
[117] Gopdchild (2004), 146.

that it had to be done and it does have to be done, but that we become committed to it as the way to save the country and the peace appears to me full of dangers,"[118]

At a special GAC meeting in Washington over the last weekend of October 1949, called to discuss the H-bomb, feelings ran high. James Conant, the veteran Washington insider, said: "We believe the super bomb should never be built."

A minority annex by Rabi and Fermi talked about genocide: "The destructiveness of this weapon makes its very existence and the knowledge of its construction a danger to humanity as a whole. It is necessarily an evil thing seen in any light."[119]

They said nobody could use a bomb a thousand times bigger than the bomb that landed on Hiroshima. The super would devastate hundreds of square miles, killing everyone. "The use of such a weapon cannot be justified on any ethical grounds which gives a human being a certain individuality and dignity, even if he happens to be a resident of an enemy country."[120] The GAC's formal recommendation was clear: "We believe the Super bomb should never be produced."[121] Teller was soon back in Washington seeing Senator Brian McMahon, the chair of the Joint Committee on Atomic Energy. "It makes me sick," said McMahon.[122] When he finally saw a copy of the GAC's report, Teller was "morose and silent". Then he bet John Manley, the physicist who was GAC secretary, that he would be imprisoned by the Russians in five years' time if they failed to build the super.

The trouble was that, as anyone who has worked in government knows, moral arguments are not terribly useful. "You know I listened as carefully as I knew how, but I don't know what Oppie

---

[118] Goodchild (2004), 147-8.

[119] Goodchild (2004), 151-3.

[120] Kunetka (1982), 156-7. From the minutes of the General Advisory Committee (1949).Washington DC: Department of Energy, Oct 30, 159.

[121] Goodchild (2004), 151.

[122] Goodchild (2004), 153.

was trying to say," said Acheson. "How can you persuade a paranoid adversary to disarm by example?"[123]

**

Strauss was now a member of the AEC, but he was acting independently, sending a report in answer to the GAC directly to Truman, and staying in close touch with Teller. It's a bad idea to "renounce unilaterally any weapon which an enemy might reasonably be expected to possess," he wrote to the president.[124]

Two weeks before the GAC's weekend away, Strauss had finally heard about the spy at Los Alamos.

Klaus Fuchs had joined from the UK when he came over with Peierls. He had stayed in the USA until 1946, and had taken part in some of Tellers's discussions about the super. He was also the main reason – though not the only one – that the bomb had come as no surprise to Stalin. Strauss must also have been wondering whether there were others.

After Fuchs was arrested in London in January, Lilienthal's meeting with Truman about the H-bomb only took seven minutes. The news that there had been a Soviet spy in Los Alamos was the final straw, and it made 1950 the height of the Cold War.

Given the prevailing atmosphere, it is hardly surprising that Truman announced a few days later that they would be building the super after all. At the end of January 1950, two weeks after news of Fuchs' arrest emerged from London, Truman made his decision.

"I have directed the Atomic Energy Commission to continue its work on all forms of atomic weapons," he said, "including the so-called hydrogen or super-bomb... until a satisfactory plan for international control of atomic energy is achieved."[125]

"I never forgave Truman," said Rabi later. "He simply did not

---

[123] Goodchild (2004), 155.
[124] Strauss (1963), 219-222.
[125] Kunetka (1928), 162.

understand what it was about … For him to have alerted the world that we were going to make a hydrogen bomb at a time when we didn't even know how to make one was one of the worst things he could have done."[126]

Three days later, the details emerged from Fuchs's questioning in London. Then, later that week, Senator Joe McCarthy made his first accusation that there were 205 'known communists' working in the state department.

The paranoia of the Cold War was going into a deep freeze. Teller predicted, as soon as he heard the news about Fuchs, that there would be a witch hunt. He was quite right.

---

[126] Goodchild (2004), 157.

Chapter 15: Creating the H-bomb

One of the many problems with the super was that Teller and Stan Ulam, the mathematician on his team at Los Alamos, didn't get on. By 1950, Ulam had written a report filled with calculations which explained how it was just not going to work.

Teller was predictably furious. He felt that Ulam was deliberately trying to undermine his project and he began to see conspiracies everywhere – and Oppenheimer's hands behind them.

Teller was frustrated by his figures. Nor could he work out and most of the rest of the staff of Los Alamos were so cross with him for his politicising.

Worse still, Ulam's calculations were backed by Fermi. Von Neumann, the computer pioneer, ran Ulam's figures through his ENIAC computer at Princeton, and came to the same conclusion.

Teller was now relying on the next Eniwetok Atoll test due in the summer of 1951 – to show that the principle worked at all. Specifically, the test codenamed 'George'. He was also cross with Oppenheimer's successor Bradley for stopping work on the super, but they could perhaps use data from the test.

**

In June 1950, the gung-ho head of the US Strategic Bomber Command, Curtis leMay, wanted to prosecute the Korean War – which began that month – by getting up there and bombing the five biggest North Korean towns to pieces. His colleagues managed to control him.

There were two tests coming up at Eniwetok Atoll. George was a fission bomb with a fusion core – a cylinder capsule with a mixture of deuterium and tritium. "Like using a blast furnace to light a match," said one scientist.

Teller was put to work chairing the committee in charge. By the middle of 1950, he had 35 scientists working full-time on the super. It still wasn't going well. Opponents of the project hoped that the nuclear tests in Eniwetok would fail to burn the deuterium effectively. Oppenheimer was hoping the idea would then die a natural death.

He was keen instead on developing small battlefield nuclear weapons, and some of these were due to be tested at the same time as George the following summer.

The Long-Range Planning Committee, chaired by Oppenheimer, reported at the end of 1950, saying that Los Alamos should concentrate on smaller weapons for the time being. Oppie had included Alvarez on the committee as a way of including the opinions of Teller and Lawrence – and he spoke up for them. But he also signed the final report. When Teller tracked him down and demanded to know why, he said he had been outmanoeuvred. Teller regarded this as more evidence for the peculiar background power of Oppenheimer.

In 1951, they arrested Fuchs's contact, Harry Gold, who led them to the Rosenbergs, arrested in Washington.

It was at this crucial moment that Ulam came up with the idea that was to make an H-bomb possible. He realised that radiation from a fission bomb could be contained and could then compress the thermonuclear material to ignite an explosion.

May 1951 saw the George test at Eniwetok. It caused a massive explosion of about 225 kilotons. Teller had been testing a mixture of tritium and deuterium, in a canister a mere 20 feet long. For a couple of seconds, it reached a temperature of 500,000 degrees – which was hotter than the sun. The technology was clearly "technically sweet," said Oppenheimer.[127]

By now the scientists at Los Alamos were very unhappy with each other. Teller decided to leave, imagining a new laboratory paid for by the US Air Force in Boulder, Colorado. He also realised that they would need six new reactors just to produce all the materials they would need. As it was, the Livermore laboratory opened in 1952, with Teller's former student and protégé Herb

---

[127] Goodchild (2004), 189.

York as the director. It was funded federally, and was set up with help from Ernest Lawrence from Berkeley.

Oppenheimer, Lilienthal and Conant failed to stop the Mike test going ahead just as people were voting – it had vaporised the island of Elugelab and created a massive fireball four miles wide, which incinerated every living thing between what had been the island and its neighbours. At 10.4 megatons, it was about twice as big as expected.

The election was won by a landslide by Dwight Eisenhower, who was a Republican – the first Republican in the White House since Hoover, two decades before – but as the former supreme allied commander in the West, he had always been sceptical about bombing people from the air with nuclear weapons. He knew Oppenheimer and broadly agreed with him.

**

Two months into Eisenhower's presidency, Stalin died – and was succeeded by an uneasy combination of Georgi Malenkov and Nikita Khruschev. The key question for us now is whether we all missed an opportunity to prevent the nuclear meltdown that still threatens us, as Oppenheimer's friend MacGeorge Bundy argued later.[128]

Malenkov and Khruschev both expressed unexpected horror at the idea of Mutual Assured Destruction (MAD). "I didn't sleep for several days," wrote Khruschev after receiving his first nuclear briefing. "I became convinced that we could never use these weapons."[129]

But at the same time, the American military establishment were so horrified at the power of the Mike test that some of them were desperate for someone to take charge.

Oppenheimer's final report for Dean Acheson's disarmament

---

[128] Macgeorge Bundy (1982), 'The missed chance to stop the H-bomb'. *New York Review of Books*, May 13, 16.
[129] Bird & Sherwin (2009), 452.

panel, which also went to Eisenhower's officials, urged "candour" – direct continual communication with the Soviets – so that they knew the size and nature of the American nuclear arsenal, and that Washington wanted to reduce its size. As it was, Washington became increasingly nervous that the Russians were ahead of them – as in fact, they very nearly were, thanks to brilliant scientists like Andrei Sakharov, their first H-bomb was tested only nine months behind Teller's.

Unfortunately for us, the world was on an inevitable path towards mutual destruction many times over. Nothing seemed able to stop it. And one of the main symptoms was the paranoid fear of each other, represented partly by a home-grown senator called Joseph McCarthy.

Chapter 16: The Crucible

Senator Joe McCarthy, a Republican Senator from Wisconsin, first came to the attention of the American public with a speech in West Virginia in February 1950, where he claimed he had a list of 205 known communists working in the State Department. Later, he lost his nerve, and the list went down to 81. He made the speech on 9 February 1950, less than a fortnight after the revelations about Fuchs and the Soviet bomb.

The speech marked the apotheosis of a collective insanity which gripped Washington in those years, starting with Truman's 1947 Federal Employees Loyalty Programme, which led to review boards who decided how 'American' federal government employees were. It also required them all to take an oath of loyalty to the US government.

The resulting blacklists and the idea that anyone was 'Un-American' led to more than 2,700 dismissals and 12,000 resignations from the years 1947 to 1956. [130] The House Committee on Un-American Activities (HUAC) was also set up during the Truman administration as a response to allegations by Republicans of disloyalty in Truman's administration.

With McCarthy in the chair, the HUAC particularly wanted to investigate the entertainment industry in Hollywood. They interrogated actors, writers, and producers. The people who cooperated in the investigations were allowed to carry on working as they had been, but people who refused to cooperate were 'blacklisted'.

McCarthy stirred up further fear of communists infiltrating the country by saying that communist spies were everywhere and that he was America's only salvation. Occasionally, he would repeat his allegations about the State Department and the US Army.

---

[130] Landon R. Y. Storrs (2015), 'McCarthyism and the Second Red Scare'. *Oxford Research Encyclopedia of American History.*

DAVID BOYLE

Playwright Arthur Miller wrote his interpretation of the Salem witch trials in 1692, *The Crucible,* as a creative response to what America was doing to itself. One baseball team, the Cincinnati Reds, even re-named themselves the 'Cincinnati Redlegs' temporarily to avoid the money-losing and career-ruining connotations inherent in being ball-playing 'Reds'.

By 1954, McCarthy began to overreach himself. After accusing the army, including war heroes, McCarthy lost credibility in the eyes of the American public. His Army-McCarthy hearings were held from March that year, and after them, he was formally censured by his colleagues in Congress. By then, it was too late for many people who were caught up in the craziness. These included Oppenheimer.

It also – again inspired by McCarthy – included a so-called 'lavender scare'. This concentrated in allegations of homosexuality – which led directly to the suicide of Alan Turing, the British computer pioneer, in Manchester, in June 1954. So, these events mattered to science too.

In fact, it was the suicide of Wyoming senator Lester Hunt because of the arrest of his son in Washington, for importuning an off-duty policeman, which really began to shift congressional opinion. It transpired that McCarthy was among those politicians who had been blackmailing him to prevent him from standing again. After that, McCarthy faded out. He began drinking heavily, though he carried on warning against communism until his death at the age of 48, just three years later, of hepatitis.

But in the early fifties, he was still a fearsome figure. During a 15-month period, 83 people refused to answer his questions about subversion on constitutional grounds and their names were made public. Nine others invoked the Fifth Amendment to the US constitution – and their names were kept quiet.

It was becoming increasingly dangerous for anyone who wanted to shift the US in more peaceful directions – as Oppenheimer did..

**

At that stage, the US Air Force was the agency charged with

delivering nuclear bombs to targets and they were particularly cross that Oppenheimer was involved in defence policy at all. In fact, he hardly was by then. The year 1952 saw a presidential election, with Eisenhower snapping at Truman's heels.

In his report to Truman, after his resignation as chair of the GAC, Oppenheimer said: "This atomic armament, which is now held to be the shield of the free world, may in a foreseeable time become the gravest threat to our welfare and security."[131]

In *Foreign Affairs*, in an article in July 1952, which he had submitted to Truman's office for approval, he came up with the image of the two scorpions:

"The atomic clock ticked faster and faster. We may anticipate a state of affairs in which two great powers will each be in a position to put an end to the civilisation and life of the other, though not without risking its own. We may be likened to two scorpions in a battle, each capable of killing the other, but only at the risk of his own life... This prospect does not make for serenity."[132]

The Eisenhower administration took office in 1953. Oppenheimer was not reappointed as consultant to the Department of Defense and Strauss was appointed to chair the Atomic Energy Commission, the AEC. One of the first things he did was to ask for the security file on Oppenheimer.

Oppie was still a consultant to the AEC, much to the rage of Strauss and some of the more gung-ho USAF officers – though he had only billed for six days over the previous year.

Four days later, Strauss moved to remove all the classified documents still in Oppenheimer's possession in Princeton.

---

[131] Richard Hewlett and Francis Duncan (1972), *A History of the United States Atomic Energy Commisison, Vol II: Atomic shield 1947-52.* Washington DC: USAEC Technical Info Centre, 518-20. Quoted in Kunetka (1982), 189.

[132] Robert Oppenheimer (1953), 'Atomic weapons and American policy', *Foreign Affairs*, July. Quoted in Kunetka (1982), 196.

DAVID BOYLE

**

In the autumn of 1953, Robert and Kitty Oppenheimer went to London to give the Reith lectures on the BBC and then onto Paris. When he reached home again before Christmas, there was a message waiting for him to call Strauss.

What happened was that one of the USAF officers, William Borden, had devoted a great deal of time to going through Oppenheimer's FBI file. Borden had flown Bombers in the war and had once seen a V2 rocket pass him – it was an experience he was never to forget: the combination of rockets and nuclear weapons. After the war, he wrote a book called *There Will Not Be Time.* As assistant to the chair of the Joint Committee on Atomic Energy, he had also become obsessed with what he saw as Oppenheimer's intransigence.

Encouraged by Strauss, his letter to the FBI detailed all their suspicions about Oppenheimer.

Borden's letter found its way to Herbert Brownell, the US Attorney General, who had just been criticising the Truman administration for promoting Harry Dexter White in the Treasury Department – the chief American negotiator at Bretton Woods – despite evidence that he was a Soviet spy.

In early December, Strauss took Borden's letter to Eisenhower. The president responded by ordering a blank wall between Oppenheimer and any more secret information, until he could be cleared. A week later, the FBI delivered a 30-inch-thick file on Oppenheimer. The result was a list of 28 charges against him – some of them true, some of them false – and most of them about things that had been long since investigated in the past. But the last four were an accusation that he had tried to delay work on the H-bomb.

Oppenheimer first met his accusers about this when they met at the headquarters of the AEC at 3.30pm on Monday 21 December 1953. Strauss also had with him the AEC's general manager, General Kenneth Nichols – who had been Groves's deputy at the Manhattan project.

Strauss told Oppenheimer that he had been forced to reassess his background under an executive order from Eisenhower about the loyalty of federal employees.

He handed over an eight-page letter, setting out the charges against him. They included his brother's membership of the communist party. Also, that he had tried to stop and delay the development of the H-bomb.

What could he do? He could just resign, which he assumed must be what they wanted, but that would be regarded as an admission of guilt – or he could request a hearing. He said he would decide later.

From the AEC offices, he went straight round to his friend, the lawyer Joseph Volpe, AEC's former general counsel. He also went to see his old friend Herbert Marks, who was currently AEC's general counsel. He decided he could not simply resign.

"This I cannot do," he wrote. "If I was this unworthy, I could hardly have served our country as I have tried, or been the director of our Institute in Princeton, or have spoken, as on more than one occasion I have found myself speaking, in the name of our science and our country."[133]

**

The AEC hired an aggressive, young lawyer, Robert Robb, with a reputation for cross-examination. For Oppenheimer, Volpe found the distinguished civil liberties lawyer Lloyd Garrison – though both Marks and Kitty felt they really wanted someone with more trial experience. But Garrison promised to find someone. In the end, he couldn't.

As the time for the hearing approached, it was clear that Robb and the three-man board were ensconced together rather a lot. Can I come too? asked Garrison. Nichols said no. Oppie's legal team

---

[133] Philip M. Stern and Harold P. Green (1969), *The Oppenheimer Case: Security on trial.* New York: Harper & Row, 229-232. Quoted in Kunetka (1982), 200.

were constantly told that this was not a trial or a court of law —
so the usual arrangements did not apply. Equally, though, because
he was not on trial, Oppenheimer would also have to prove his
innocence.

For example, and unknown to them, since his first meeting with
Volpe and Marks, his conversations with his lawyers had all been
secretly recorded and given to Robb and the panel.

Then there was the issue of security clearance for his legal team.
Robb's security clearance went through eight days, but Garrison
was told that he was the only one who could be cleared. In that
case, the team decided none of them would be cleared. There was
then the prospect that Oppenheimer would be represented alone in
court, when anything was discussed that touched on national
security. For example, they realised they really needed the minutes
of the GAC committee in October 1949 – an official secret – where
they had presided over the discussion of the H-bomb. But they
weren't allowed to see them.

Realising this, Garrison belatedly applied for security clearance
on March 26, but at the end of April – five weeks later – there was
still no sign of it.

Just before the hearing opened, Oppenheimer ran into a friend in
Washington DC and said that he and Kitty were, by then, "in real
trouble".

That was no less than the truth.

Chapter 17: The Trial

The first time they cleared the courtroom because national security was involved – set up in a long room in Room 2022 in Building T-3, the AEC's temporary office near the Washington monument – it was on the second day of the hearings. It was during the cross-examination of one of Oppenheimer's former colleagues, Mervin Kelly, now president of the Bell telephone company.

Had he written a report with Oppenheimer? Did it mention thermonuclear weapons? "I don't think so," said Kelly.

"I should like to read the witness something … from a report that is classified," said Robb. Then the room was cleared and Oppenheimer's whole legal team were forced to leave him alone in there.

They were on a table shaped like a U, with the rival legal teams facing each other across the two legs and the board of inquiry at the top. There was a chair for witnesses in front of them and behind it, was a sofa, where Kitty sat – her leg in plaster after she fell down a flight of steps – and where Oppenheimer chain-smoked, when he was not giving evidence.

Throughout this strange hearing, three men sat in judgement. They were:

• Gordon Gray, the chair of this Personnel Security Board and president of the University of North Carolina.
• Thomas Morgan, former president of Sperry Gyroscope & Co.
• Ward Evans, chair of the chemistry department of Northwestern University.

At lunchtime on the first day, 12 April, Garrison phoned James Reston from the *New York Times* and authorised him to go ahead with their story – they had leaked him the original AEC letter and Oppie's reply.

So, the next morning, when the Oppenheimer team was late

again and the case was splashed across the front pages of the papers, Gray was extremely irritated – he had only the day before assured everyone that the proceedings were confidential.

Then Oppenheimer was in the hot seat through most of April 13 and he was cross-examined by Robb on the third day, a Wednesday. By the afternoon they had reached the Chevalier affair. It was immediately clear to everyone that Robb had access to a transcript of a recording of Oppenheimer's interview with Colonel Pash, 11 years before. Instead, Oppenheimer had to rely on his own memory.

"Did you tell Pash that x had approved three persons on the project?" asked Robb.

"I'm not clear whether I said that there were three or that x had approached other people…"

Robb consulted his transcript. "Didn't you say that x had approached people?"

"Probably," said Oppenheimer, bowing to the inevitable.

"Why did you do that, doctor?" asked Robb.

"Because I was an idiot."[134]

His answers took longer to arrive and became increasingly faint. He sat with his head bowed, as white as a sheet and with his hands between his knees. This was clearly serious.

"Isn't it a fair statement today, Dr Oppenheimer," asked Robb, "that according to your testimony now, you told not one lie to Colonel Pash, but a whole fabric and a tissue of lies?"

To this, Oppenheimer replied simply: "Right."[135]

Next, he had to go through the ordeal of being questioned about his visit to see Jean Tatlock in June 1943, when she was a known communist and he was doing important and highly secret war work. This was after all, in his third year of marriage to Kitty, who was sitting just behind him.

"Did you find out why *she* had to see you?" Robb asked.

"Because she was still in love with me."

---

[134] Kunitka (1982), 228.
[135] Goodchild (1980), 241.

Robb even forced him to confirm that he had spent the night with her.

"You don't think that spending the night with a dedicated communist…?"

"I don't believe she was a dedicated communist."[136]

When he got home at midnight that night, Robb told his wife: "I've just seen a man destroy himself on the witness stand."[137]

Robb was giving Strauss daily reports from what was happening in the hearing and Strauss passed it onto the President: "On Wednesday, Oppenheimer admitted, under oath, that he had lied… An extremely bad impression towards Oppenheimer had already developed in the minds of the board," wrote Strauss.[138]

**

There then followed a succession of up to 30 witnesses for Oppenheimer's character. They began with Groves, who said that he had done "a magnificent job at Los Alamos".[139] But, when Robb asked him if he would clear him today, he had to say that "under this interpretation," he probably wouldn't.[140] The nation was a different place to what it had been a decade before, after all.

In they all came, his former colleagues, to exonerate him – Von Neumann, Lilienthal, Rabi, and a range of others. Rabi said: "I think he has always been a loyal American. There was no doubt in my mind about that. But he has learned more about the way you have to live in the world as it is now. We hope at some future time that the carefree days will return."[141]

Then followed Robb's own witnesses, notably Edward Teller.

It was still not quite clear whose side Teller would be on. Given

---

[136] Kunetka, (1982), 229.
[137] Goodchild (1980), 242.
[138] Bird & Swinton (2008), 514.
[139] Kunetka (1982), 230.
[140] Kunetka (1982), 239
[141] Kunetka (1982), 237.

that he was never questioning Oppenheimer's loyalty, Oppie asked him to come to Washington to meet his lawyers. He came and spent half an hour with Garrison. Then he went to see Robb, who asked him to read a transcript of Oppenheimer's testimony. So, in the end, Teller testified against. He said the Chevalier affair had just been a misunderstanding. He never questioned Oppenheimer's loyalty. Yes, but would you restore his security clearance, Gray asked Teller on the witness chair?

"I believe that is merely a question of belief," said Teller. "And there is no expertness, no real information, behind it, that Dr Oppenheimer's character is such that he would not knowingly and willingly do anything that is designed to endanger the safety of this country – to that extent, I would say that I do not see any reasons to deny clearance."

Then he shifted his position, and fatally undermined Oppenheimer's case:

"If it is a question of wisdom and judgement, as understood by actions since 1945, then I would say one would be wiser not to grant clearance. I must say that I am myself a little bit confused on this issue, particularly as it refers to a person of Dr Oppenheimer's prestige and influence. May I limit myself to these comments?"[142]

Ernest Lawrence set out from Berkeley to testify against Oppenheimer, but – on the way there – had such a bad attack of colitis that he went back to California, where he died four years later.

This led to a major row with Strauss who called him a coward for his failure to show up.

The problem for Strauss and his fellow accusers was that Oppenheimer was clearly no spy. That accusation had been around since 1939 – if he had been, what were Eltenton and Chevalier doing approaching him for information so subtly and so carefully?

As for the evidence from the air force officers, about his failure

---

[142] Bernstein (1984), 164.

to be even-handed about the possibilities of naval propulsion and nuclear-powered planes – then the mere thought of such terrifying monstrosities should be enough to have dampened anyone's enthusiasm for what they were saying.

On 6 May, when the hearings ended, Gray felt pretty pleased with himself, and went on holiday for ten days. When he came back, he was appalled to find – not just that Strauss had decided to give the transcript to the press – but that Evans had gone over to the other side. He was determined to clear Oppenheimer and to restore his security clearance.

When he heard this, Strauss panicked and begged the FBI to intervene and talk individually to his board. Probably wisely, FBI boss J. Edgar Hoover decided that could be counter-productive.

That was why the panel of judges agreed that Oppenheimer was indeed a loyal citizen. But they went on:

"We have however been unable to arrive at the conclusion that it would be consistent with the security of the United States to reinstate Dr Oppenheimer's clearance. Therefore, we do not so recommend...

"1. We find that his continuing conduct and associations reflected a serious disregard for the requirements of security.

2. A susceptibility to influence which could have serious implications for security.

3. His conduct in the H-bomb debate raises a doubt whether his future participation would be in the best interests of security.

4. We have regretfully concluded that Dr Oppenheimer has been less than candid in several instances in his testimony before this board."[143]

Evans – who they had assumed would be biased against Oppenheimer because of his Jewish heritage – had, ironically enough, asked Robb to improve his prose (and he had agreed to

---

[143] Bird & Sherwin (2008), 541.

help so that Evans would not like a 'placeman'):

"Most of the derogatory information was in the hands of the committee when Dr Oppenheimer was cleared in 1947. They apparently were aware of his associations and his left-wing politics; yet they cleared him. They took a chance because of his special talents and he continued to do a good job. Now when the job is done, we are asked to investigate him on practically the same derogatory information. There is not the slightest vestige of information before this Board that would indicate that he is not a loyal citizen of this country. He hates Russia. He had communistic friends, it is true. He still has some. However, the evidence is that he has fewer of them than he did in 1947… I personally think that our failure to clear Dr Oppenheimer will be a black mark on the escutcheon of this country. His witnesses were a considerable segment of the scientific backbone of our Nation and they endorse him…"[144]

As a final shot, Nichols still had to write up a recommendation to the AEC board. So he added in his report a charge of perjury – presumably with Strauss' agreement – related to the Chevalier business: this meant turning around the order of events a little. As if Oppenheimer had told the truth to Pash and then had lied instead to the hearing. There was no evidence for that at all. Garrison would undoubtedly have objected if he had seen the document – but he wasn't allowed to see it.

One of the problems of not letting the defendant see their own documentation – as Robb did with Oppenheimer – is that it can be harder to get to the truth. It might have jogged his memory. Because there were, in fact, three scientists that Eltenton was trying to contact – Oppenheimer, Lawrence and Alvarez. So maybe it had not actually been quite the 'tissue of lies' that Oppenheimer had admitted to. Though it wasn't clear where he had heard this – perhaps it was from Chevalier himself.

---

[144] Bird & Sherwin (2008), 541-2.

Nor was any attempt made to reach either Chevalier (living in Paris) or Eltenton (living in England).

**

By the end of June, Strauss was clear that he had all the votes of his five commissioners, except one: the scientist and Manhattan project official historian Henry Smyth. "Lewis, the difference between you and me is that you see everything in either black or white and to me everything looks grey," said Smyth, after lunch with Strauss to talk it through.

"Harry," said Strauss, quick as a flash. "Let me recommend you to a good oculist."[145]

Smyth wrote his dissenting opinion, only to find that Strauss had rewritten his comments to counter it. So, with it due early the following morning, he worked through the night. As he worked, he could see two men outside his house watching him. He assumed they had been sent to intimidate him, by either the AEC or the FBI. "You know," he said to his assistant, "it's funny that I should be going to all this trouble for Oppenheimer. I don't even like the guy much."[146]

At 7 the next morning, his assistant took it around to the AEC and waited to make sure it was distributed in full.

So it was that Oppenheimer's security clearance was withdrawn when it only had one day still to run.

**

It is difficult to imagine what it must have been like to go through an ordeal like that – the physical strain – without knowing, as we do now, that the world would escape annihilation, anyway for a while, and that the stifling atmosphere of treason and suspicion would lift – slowly, but that sanity was going to prevail

---

[145] Bird & Sherwin (2008), 545.
[146] *Ibid,*

again. Harry Dexter White had, after all, collapsed after giving evidence at his hearing in Congress in 1948, and died two days later.

To some, Oppie seemed his old self, but occasionally the full horror was clear – his hair had gone white during the hearing. "Much of his previous spirit and liveliness left him," said Bethe.

His friend Robert Serber said that, after the hearings, he was "a sad man and his spirit was broken".

"I think to a certain extent it actually almost killed him, spiritually, yes," said Rabi. "It achieved what his opponents wanted to achieve; it destroyed him."[147]

His security clearance was never given back.

---

[147] Bird & Sherwin (2008), 552.

Chapter 18: Afterwards

After his ordeal was over, Oppenheimer offered to resign from leading the Institute for Advanced Study in Princeton in July 1954. But they held a special governors' meeting and decided not to let him go – after the whole teaching faculty signed a petition calling on him to stay.

Strauss found it all deeply frustrating.

It was the first sign of a backlash – and especially from the scientific community. And especially on 6 June. This was, by coincidence, also the day that Alan Turing killed himself in Manchester, probably after being browbeaten by security staff (who didn't want him repeating a holiday near the Soviet border with his Norwegian boyfriend).[148] This was the day when Strauss decided to hand the transcripts over to the press, using the excuse that a member of his board had left his copy on a train (though actually it had been handed back almost straight away).

This was especially tough on Teller. "The exile I was to undergo at the hands of my fellow physicists, akin to the shunning practised by some religious groups, began almost as soon as the testimony was released," he wrote later:[149] "My recollection of that painful period is general rather than specific: I was more miserable than I had ever been before in my entire life."

When Teller next visited Los Alamos, he put out his hand to greet a friend – a former housemate – and "he looked me coldly in the eye, refused my hand, and turned away. I was so stunned that for a moment I couldn't react. Then I realised that my life as I had known it was over. I took Mici by the arm, and we retreated to our

---

[148] David Boyle (2014), *Alan Turing: Unlocking the Enigma.* London: Sharpe books, https://www.amazon.co.uk/Alan-Turing-Unlocking-David-Boyle-ebook/dp/B07B5PRZDD/
[149] Quoted in Goodchild (2004), 249.

room upstairs."[150]

Back inside his room, he wept.

"If a person leaves his country, leaves his Continent, leaves his relatives, leaves his friends, the only people he knows are business professional colleagues," said Teller. "If more than 90 percent of them come around to consider him an enemy, an outcast, it is bound to have an effect. The truth is it had a profound effect, it affected Mici, it affected her health."[151]

He asked Strauss to make some kind of statement that he never meant that he wanted to limit people's opinions. Strauss asked Robb to reply.

In fact, the press was mostly sympathetic to him – but it was all so embarrassing. When James Shepley of *Time* magazine wrote a book called *The Hydrogen Bomb, the Men, the Menace and the Mechanism,* it disparaged Oppenheimer and Bradbury, and implied that the whole idea had been fully formed inside Teller's head.

He went to see Fermi, who was dying in hospital and asked his advice about something he had written to set the record straight. "According to Enrico," said a friend afterwards. "Edward talked non-stop about the effects of the hearing. He was so emotionally overwrought at the time that Enrico thought he was close to suicide."[152]

When Enrico Fermi died, Teller lost his oldest and closest friend in physics.

**

Strauss was not finished with Oppenheimer yet. He even went to the UK to warn Lord Cherwell, scientific advisor to Prime

---

[150] *Ibid.*
[151] Stanley Bumberg & Gwinn Owen (1976), *Integrity and Conflict.* New York: GPutnam & Sons, 365. Quoted in Goodchild (2004), 250.
[152] Goodchild (2004), 255.

Minister Churchill and the chair of the UK Atomic Energy Authority, that it would be 'unwise' for Bristol university to offer him a job.

It was not until October that the FBI withdrew their surveillance of him – he had been watched through the family's summer holiday in the US Virgin Islands, because of 'inside knowledge' that he was about to defect to the Russians. Herb Marks advised Oppenheimer to tell Hoover and the FBI wherever he was going.

But the FBI tails found that they couldn't always follow him on holiday – he and Kitty and their two children were sailing – so, at the airport in New York on their way home, he was accosted by FBI men again and asked to go with them to a private room. He agreed, on condition that Kitty came too.

There they asked him point blank if he had been approached by any Russians.

Richard Crossman in London's *New Statesman,* the leftist weekly, asked: "How can the independent experimental mind survive in such an atmosphere?"

In Paris, Haakon Chevalier read sections of the transcripts, sent to him by Oppenheimer, to his friend André Malraux, the French novelist and culture minister. "The trouble was," said Malraux, "he accepted his accusers' terms from the beginning… He should have told them from the very outset: 'Je suis la bombe atomique!'"[153]

**

Strauss never stopped trying to undermine him and catch him out.

In the years that followed, he was involved in Eisenhower's 'Atoms for Peace' programme. Guided by Strauss, the navy took up nuclear energy as a tool to power submarines. The first pressurised water reactor or PWR was in the submarine *Nautilus* by 1955. The first reactor which was primarily designed to provide

---

[153] Bird & Sherwin (2008), 556.

electricity – rather than to produce materials for bombs – was organised by the navy (thanks to Admiral Strauss) at Shippingport, Pennsylvania, and began working in May 1955.

It was that year, in fact, that Strauss was unwise enough to make the prediction that the future of energy would be "too cheap to meter".

It hasn't proved to have been that way – partly because of the enormous and increasing set up costs, partly because of the risks of terrorists getting hold of plutonium – but also because of the cost of managing the nuclear waste.

In February 1955, the AEC published their report on their Bravo test, which talked about the fallout in a cigar shape, 220 miles long and covering 7,000 square miles. It was the first time that the term 'strontium -90' came to the public's attention.

Strontium-90 was an isotope of strontium which is one of the main elements of fallout from nuclear testing. Concern was rising across the world that new born babies would absorb strontium-90 into their bones – up to the 'baby tooth' survey of children born in St Louis, Missouri which showed that, in 1963, they had levels in their teeth 50 times higher than children born in 1950, before large scale nuclear testing began.[154]

One of the great opponents of atmospheric testing was Joseph Rotblat, a Polish physicist who had left Los Alamos after the collapse of Nazi Germany. He was by then living in the UK.

Partly because of the concern about strontium-90, and partly because Churchill was prime minister again from 1951 – and he was pressing successfully for the USA to implement his Hyde Park agreement with Roosevelt from 1943 for sharing nuclear know-how (Congress had never seen a copy!).

Rotblat was among the public figures in the UK who founded the Campaign for Nuclear Disarmament in 1957 in London, which was to have a major influence on the peace movement in the UK. They organised peaceful marches every Easter from 1958 to 1965 outside the Aldermaston nuclear defence research establishment.

---

[154] https://en.wikipedia.org/wiki/Baby_Tooth_Survey

CND was launched by Canon John Collins, philosopher Bertrand Russell and peace activist Peggy Duff.

Russell and Szilard had invited Oppenheimer to the inaugural Pugwash conference, in Pugwash, Nova Scotia – launched in July 1955 with a 'manifesto' signed by Russell, Einstein (his last public act) and eight others – but he declined. He didn't want to step out of line – he preferred to prove himself a reliable patriot.

In his Livermore laboratory, Teller was responding to the growing opposition to atmospheric tests by developing a 'clean' bomb with no fallout. But the rest of the time, he was busy lobbying the government to head off the push towards the Test Ban treaty.

Livermore's Bassoon Test in 1956 saw 17,000 miles of fallout across the Pacific, although it was nominally a 'clean' bomb – which is why Strauss called it 'humanitarian'. Physicist Ralph Lapp wrote an article for the *Bulletin of Atomic Scientists* that 'cleanliness' is a relative term': "Part of the madness of our time is that an adult man can use the word 'humanitarian' to describe the H-bomb."[155]

The missionary theologian Albert Schweizer used his Nobel Peace Prize acceptance speech to condemn the practice of atmospheric testing in 1957. The chemist Linus Pauling launched a petition among scientists against testing – 200 of them signed. An elderly couple living near the Nevada test site wrote to Eisenhower to tell him that one of their children was slowly dying of leukaemia. He was appalled.

Eisenhower heard that the Russians were keen for a test ban and he responded. He managed to hold out against Strauss and the chairman of the joint chiefs of staff, Admiral Arthur Radford. At the end of June 1957, Strauss finally stepped down as the chair of the AEC, which meant that Teller had lost an ally.

Scientists were now negotiating with the Russians, and they were making progress. They recommended 160 posts to be set up around the world to listen for the slightest sound of a test.

---

[155] Goodchild (2004), 267.

Underground tests were a particular problem, but Eisenhower was very pleased to announce a year's moratorium to start in October 1958. He proposed to Khrushchev that they make it the beginning of a permanent ban.

Teller was now part of a small group of scientific policy insiders who were trying to prevent this process from developing. Livermore was an exciting place, full of energy trying to think about how to get around the ban – not because they were planning to themselves, of course, but because they believed the Russians would.

Teller's team wrote a report based on the experimental evidence that underground tests and tests in space would be difficult to detect. Eisenhower was deeply frustrated and extended the moratorium but, before his hoped-for Paris talks could begin, the Russians arrested Gary Powers and his U2 spy plane.

So, it was a disappointed Eisenhower who left office in 1961: his only achievement in terms of nuclear non-proliferation was his phrase 'Atoms for Peace' in his speech which earned him a standing ovation at the United Nations in December 1958.

His final address to the nation in January 1961 warned that the 'military industrial complex', overseen by a scientific and technological elite – was increasingly powerful. Later, he said he was referring to Edward Teller and Werner Von Braun.[156]

**

The new President John Kennedy inherited warheads for making 18,000 nuclear weapons. Teller was by then desperately working against the ban. In the end it was the Russians that ended the moratorium, when they gave 2 days' notice that they were about to hold a test - which included a massive 58-megaton explosion, the biggest ever recorded.

It was so big, in fact, that it became impossible for Kennedy to resist carrying out a test himself.

---

[156] Goodchidld (2004), 283n.

Strauss's term as AEC chair had been completed by the end of June 1958. Eisenhower wanted to reappoint him but Strauss was afraid the senate would subject him to fierce questioning. Besides the Oppenheimer affair, he had clashed with Democrats in the senate, including over his autocratic handling of the AEC chairmanship. By this time, he had managed to develop a reputation as "one of the nation's ablest and thorniest public figures," according to *Time* magazine.[157]

Eisenhower had offered him the post of White House Chief of Staff, to replace Sherman Adams, but Strauss didn't like the idea. He also asked if Strauss would consider taking over from John Foster Dulles (who was ill) as Secretary of State. But Strauss did not want to get in the way of a friend of his. Finally, he accepted the post of commerce secretary in Eisenhower's cabinet. He took office during Senate recess for the 1958 elections, though Senate opposition to this appointment was growing. On the other hand, some commentators were surprised at the appointment given how much experience Strauss had – he even seemed a little over-qualified.

Even so, Senator Clinton Anderson, who had a long-standing feud with Strauss – allied with Senator Gale McGee on the commerce committee – to make sure he was not formally appointed. McGee charged Strauss with a "brazen attempt to hoodwink the committee" by over-stating his role in developing the H-bomb. Truman was also irritated and wrote to remonstrate with Anderson about it – and Anderson leaked the letter to the press. Strauss tried to reach Truman through an intermediary, but he was rebuffed. A group of scientists who were still angry about what Strauss had done to Oppenheimer lobbied against confirming him in post. They called themselves the 'Last Straws'.

After 16 days of hearings, the committee recommended his confirmation by one vote (9-8). But by then, it had become a *cause célèbre* and a national news story as – according to *Time* magazine

---

[157] *Time* magazine (1959), *"The Administration: The Strauss Affair"*, Jun 15..

– "the biggest, bitterest, and in many ways the most unseemly confirmation fights in senate history."[158]

On 15 June 1959, just after midnight, the full senate voted 49-46 not to approve his nomination. At the time, it was only the eighth time in US history that a cabinet appointee had not been approved by Congress. The last time it happened was in 1925, and it didn't happen again until 1989.

"I am losing a truly valuable associate in the business of government," said Eisenhower. "If the Nation is to be denied the right to have as public servants in responsible positions men of his proven character, ability and integrity, then indeed it is the American people who are the losers through this sad episode."[159]

The Senate rejection automatically removed Strauss that day from the cabinet. He never quite recovered from it.

In his autobiography, he tells some strange stories about the experience. Like when a woman sitting behind him got up suddenly and shouted: "That man Strauss financed Lenin, Trotsky and the Bolshevik revolution!"

As she was led out, one of the senators said *sotto voce*: "Must have been in knee pants when he did all that financing."[160]

"Those of you who have been long associated with me in public life know I speak the truth," he said at the end of the hearings, when he had the chance to speak for himself. "Some who have testified against me, or have given notice of their intention to do so, have never even met me…"[161]

It may have been a terrible miscarriage of justice, but – either way – there were people who felt it was richly deserved.

**

[158] *Ibid,.*

[159]https://www.presidency.ucsb.edu/documents/statement-the-president-the-rejection-the-nomination-lewis-l-strauss-secretary-commerce

[160] Strauss (1963), 389.

[161] Strauss (1963), 391.

OPPENHEIMER: A WORLD DESTROYED

In 1960, Teller stepped down as director of Livermore labs, which he had taken up in 1958 when York's successor was killed in a car accident. He was persuaded to meet Kennedy and the two men spent 45 minutes together. It was clearly a strain for both of them. Teller urged him to resume nuclear testing and to build deep shelters for the whole population. Kennedy was horrified by the vision this represented.

Kennedy probably thought back to the conversation during the Cuban Missile Crisis of 1962, when – with the help of Robert McNamara – for 13 days, he had wrestled to prevent armageddon.

After that experience, he re-doubled his efforts for a test ban – and found that, wherever he turned – there was Teller, passionately briefing against the whole idea.

**

Fermi, who stayed loyal to Oppenheimer, and who gave evidence on his behalf died of stomach cancer in 1954 (two of his assistants at the Chicago pile in 1942 also died of cancer). In 1956, the AEC named their highest award after him, and Edward Teller was one of the first to get it for contributions to nuclear physics. The incident led to a row with Mici about his draft acceptance speech, as she and his friends struggled to tone it down.

But, aware that the risks of cheating were nothing compared to the bigger risk of collision course with the Soviets, Kennedy's efforts began to bear fruit, and Teller had to admit defeat. He desperately wanted acceptance, so he recommended that his successor for the $50,000 Fermi Prize should be Oppenheimer.

It was hardly straightforward, because the day that Kennedy announced he would be presenting it, he was shot dead. The new president Lyndon Johnson gave it to him instead. "I think it's just possible Mr President, that it has taken some charity and some courage to make this award today," Oppenheimer said in response. "That would seem to be a good augury for all our futures."[162]

---

[162] Bird & Sherwin (2008), 574.

It was an important moment. Teller had hoped that suggesting that Oppenheimer should get the award would lead to a reconciliation. They shook hands, willingly, though – judging by the look on Kitty's face – not too happily.

In December 1965, Oppenheimer agreed to step down as director of the Institute for Advanced Study, on condition that they build him a house next door to his new library.

He commissioned an architect, but Strauss used his influence as a board member behind the scenes to get them to take back their promise. That decision was reversed again and the house was built from 1966, but Oppenheimer would never live in it.

He was already sick with the throat cancer that would kill him. He died in his sleep on 18 February 1967.

Strauss sent a cable to Kitty saying he was grieved by Robert's death.[163]

**

Kitty spent her years of widowhood in the Virgin Islands, yachting with Oppie's friend Bob Serber. She was drinking heavily, as she had done most of their married life (Strauss called it dipsomania'). "She burns with an intensity of feeling one rarely sees," wrote Lilienthal in his diary. "Mostly with deep resentment against all those who had any part in the torture Robert had to undergo."[164]

In May 1972, she bought a 50-foot yacht and persuaded Bob Server to sail around the world with her. But she became ill off the Panama coast five months later. She died of an embolism in hospital in Panama City.

Some evidence has emerged that it was Kitty not Robert who was working for the Soviets. But I suspect that this may be based on unrealistic and imaginative fantasies on the part of the Soviet spy network in the USA. We will probably never know.

---

[163] Bird & Sherwin (2008), 587.
[164] Bird & Sherwin (2008), 577-8.

OPPENHEIMER: A WORLD DESTROYED

**

Strauss had been furious that the Kennedy administration should attempt to rehabilitate Oppenheimer by giving him the Fermi award. He stirred up disaffection among the Republican congress.[165]

The commerce defeat effectively ended Strauss's government career. The numerous enemies that Strauss had made during his career took some pleasure from the turn of events. Strauss himself was deeply hurt by the rejection, and never fully recovered from it. He tended to brood over events past.

Strauss published his memoirs, *Men and Decisions*, in 1962. At the time, *Time* magazine's review said they "may now remind readers of his many real accomplishments before they were obscured by political rows."[166] The book sold well, spending fifteen weeks on the *New York Times* best seller list for non-fiction, rising as high as number five. The general view of historians is that the memoirs were self-serving.[167]

His link with Herbert Hoover stayed strong throughout the years. In 1962, Hoover wrote in a letter to Strauss: "Of all the men who have come into my orbit in life, you are the one who has my greatest affections, and I will not try to specify the many reasons, evidences or occasions."[168]

Strauss helped drum up support for Barry Goldwater in the 1964 presidential election. He also stayed on good terms with

---

[165] Strauss (1963), 153.
[166] Barton J. Bernstein (1986), 'Sacrifices and Decisions: Lewis L. Strauss', in *The Public Historian*, vol. 8, no. 2, 120. Available at https://doi.org/10.2307/3377436..
[167] *Ibid.*
[168] Sonja P. Wentling (2000), 'The Engineer and the Shtadlanim': Herbert Hoover and American Jewish non-Zionists, 1917-28', in *American Jewish History*. Vol .88, No 3: 378n2. Available at: 10.1353/ajh.2000.0058. JSTOR 23886392

Eisenhower, and – for several years in the 1960s – Eisenhower and Strauss tried to get an abortive nuclear-powered, desalination plant in the Middle East that would benefit both Israel and its Arab neighbours.

Otherwise, Strauss gave his time to philanthropic activities, and to American Jewish causes. He bought a farm in Virginia and started breeding Black Angus cattle. A book he was working on about Herbert Hoover – who had died aged 90 in 1964 – was never finished.

Strauss died of cancer on 21 January 1974, at his home in Brandy. He is buried in Richmond Hebrew Cemetery, alongside the graves 30 Jewish Confederate soldiers who died in or near Richmond, and together with more than 60 other family members.

**

After his father's death, Peter Oppenheimer moved to New Mexico and settled in Santa Fe, becoming an environmental activist. Toni never really quite recovered from her father's death. She needed security clearance for her job translating at the UN, but – all the stuff about Robert came out – and the clearance never emerged. In January 1977, she hanged herself in the cottage that Robert had built on the beach at St John in the US Virgin Islands. Hundreds of people came to her funeral.

**

Then the only one left of the three was Teller.

He found himself on the wrong side of the 1960s revolt. Bertrand Russell broke with CND as soon as 1961, when he started the Committee of 100 to organise direct action – at the age of 89 (he used to be arrested by ambulance when he took part in actions outside 10 Downing Street).

One of his last actions before he died, in 1970 when he was 97, was organising a mock tribunal for war criminals in Sweden. Berkeley students were particularly militant, and they were excited to find one of the war criminals living nearby. A jeering crowd went to Teller's house but the police in riot gear got there first.

Through his membership of organisations like Peace Through Strength, he was now a member of many right-wing and conservative groups. In fact, Teller had gained considerable power and influence. That was part of his tragedy, according to his biographer.[169]

When he was 70 in 1978, Teller talked about his obsession with building a defensive shield. But his main activity that year was supporting the beleaguered nuclear energy industry after the fire at the Harrisburg reactor in Pennsylvania. "I was the only victim of Three Mile Island," he wrote in the *Wall Street Journal* at the same time as passing comment on the nuclear conspiracy film *The China Syndrome* with Jane Fonda and Jack Lemmon.

He was describing his heart attack at that time. "No, that would be wrong," he wrote. "It was not the reactor – it was Jane Fonda. Reactors are not dangerous."[170]

Early in the 1980 presidential campaign, Ronald Reagan had been taken to Norad, the North American Aerospace Defence Command – and saw that he could watch enemy missiles rain down on the USA, but could do nothing about them. It was a salutary experience.

When he was elected, Reagan ordered a massive $1.5 trillion defence budget. A few days after the election – not entirely coincidentally – Livermore was testing their laser defence shield. According to Teller it was a great success. He called the system 'Excalibur'.

This was Teller's third generation nuclear tech – the first had been the A-bomb, then the H-bomb and then these nuclear-driven X-ray lasers.

Admiral James Watkins, the chief of naval operations, was a devout catholic – and he shared his bishops' unease at Mutual

---

[169] Goodchild (2004), 322.

[170] Goodchild (2004), 327. from *Wall Street Journal* (1978), July 31.

Assured Destruction or MAD. He met Teller in January 1983 and became a major supporter of laser defence.

Despite this, it was hard pinning down the administration to a long-term commitment for funds. Teller was constantly in Washington, talking up the idea of Excalibur and Super Excalibur, an exaggeration of the last one. The Livermore director Roy Woodruff was furious. Tests had not even shown that the lasers would be powerful enough to be used as a weapon.

Teller agreed that he had exaggerated but he refused to send a corrective letter. Consequently, Reagan went ahead with his famous Star Wars speech in 1983 – and it horrified the Russians.

When Mikhail Gorbachev took control of the Soviet Union in 1985, he found the same kind of divisions over SDI (Strategic Defence Initiative) among his own scientists as they were in the USA. Their consensus was that Star Wars was a ruse - the Americans were just looking for ways to organise the first strike of their own.

At the November 1986 Reykjavik summit, Reagan was shocked when Gorbachev offered major cuts in weaponry - on condition that they confined star wars research to the laboratory. When Reagan failed to respond, the Soviets were cross but they stayed. And Gorbachev upped his offer to get rid of 100 percent of nuclear warheads.

In December 1987, the Intermediate Nuclear Forces treaty was signed in Washington (President Trump withdrew from it in 2018 and only 4 percent of the 50,000 warheads were ever destroyed).[171] Gorbachev came to Washington for the signing and Reagan hosted a dinner in his honour.

"This is Dr Teller," said Reagan. There was no response, so Reagan repeated the introduction: "This is the famous Dr Teller."

Gorbachev still didn't move. Finally, he said: "There are many Tellers."[172]

Teller left the introduction line. "I've come to regard the

---

[171]https://www.youtube.com/watch?v=UQC7NeVS4UE
[172] Goodchild (2004), 381.

incident as a great compliment... I am a little proud that my efforts to protect freedom and to extend it to those behind the iron curtain were noticed," he wrote later.[173]

**

George Bush *père* as president from 1988 coincided with Teller's new iteration of star wars as 'brilliant pebbles'. Teller told the new administration that they would take five years to deploy 100,000 pebbles and would cost only $50 billion.

Teller wrote a paper claiming that, from its inception, the SDI was "intended to protect the whole of mankind not just a single nation."[174]

In August 1990, they tested the pebbles in space and – according to Teller – this second test was 90 percent successful. The same year, he was invited to Budapest to lecture. He loved it, and in January 1991, he went again with Mici.

By then, Teller was 84, not in the best of health, when the General Accounting Office raised concerns about the programmes from Livermore. Far from being 90 percent successful, about 90 per cent of the pebbles had failed to detect, acquire or track an accelerating target.[175]

Meanwhile, Teller was in Russia, where he met Yuli Khariton who had been head of the soviet nuclear programme. He even nominated him for the Fermi award, but this was not supported back home in the USA.

But things were changing then at home too. Within four months of taking office, the Clinton administration announced a shift in purpose of brilliant pebbles from national defence to defending forces against battlefield missiles. It was a new world, dominated by terrorism – no amount of technology would have prevented 9/11, for example.

---

[173] 161 *Ibid.*
[174] Goodchild (2004), 389-90.
[175] *Ibid.*

In 1995, Teller suffered a serious stroke. Then in 2000, Mici died, after years of dementia. "I cannot overestimate how much her steadfast love and support sustained me for 76 years, 66 of them as my wife," he said.[176]

In August 2003, he received the President's Medal of Freedom from George W. Bush Junior. A fortnight later, on 7 September 2003, he had another stroke and died two days later.

The last of that generation, Alice Strauss, lived until 2004, when she died at the age of 101, at Brandy Station.

---

[176] Goodchild (2004), 394.

OPPENHEIMER: A WORLD DESTROYED

Chapter 19: Conclusions

The Oppenheimer case quickly became a *cause célèbre* among physicists and scientists more widely, with Strauss frequently being cast in the role of villain. This was an image that would persist ever since. But he has also had his defenders as well, who saw the hero and villain roles the other way around.

Strauss was an odd mixture. Someone who interviewed him a number of times in the mid-1950s, Walter Schilling, said that he was bland and courteous in one session but prickly and temperamental in another one.[177]

His front-page obituary in the *New York Times* said: "For a dozen years at the outset of the atomic age, Lewis Strauss, an urbane but sometimes thorny former banker with a gifted amateur's knowledge of physics, was a key figure in the shaping of United States thermonuclear policy. ... In the years of his mightiest influence in Washington, the owlish-faced Mr. Strauss puzzled most observers. He was, on the one hand, a sociable person who enjoyed dinner parties and who was adept at prestidigitation; and, on the other hand, he gave the impression of intellectual arrogance. He could be warm-hearted yet seem at times like a stuffed shirt. He could make friends yet create antagonisms."[178]

Decades after he died, historians are still looking through Strauss's records and actions. Ken Young, an expert on the early Cold War period, has written about the development of the H-bomb to look at the role that Strauss played in trying to form that history to his own benefit. Young looked particularly at the

---

[177] Ken Young & Walter Schilling (2019). *Super Bomb: Organizational Conflict and the Development of the Hydrogen Bomb*. Ithaca, NY: Cornell University Press, 144.
[178] Alden Whitman (1974), 'Lewis Strauss Dies; Ex-Head of A.E.C'. *New York Times,* Jan 22, 1 & 64. Available at Archive.

publication during 1953 and 1954 of a popular magazine article and book that promoted a highly distorted notion that the hydrogen bomb project had been unreasonably stalled, both before Truman's decision and after, by a small group of American scientists working against the national interest – and that Strauss was one of the heroes who had overcome this cabal's efforts.[179]

Young found circumstantial archival evidence that Strauss was behind both publications and may well have given classified information to the book authors involved.[180]

Along the same lines, the historian Priscilla Johnson McMillan has identified archival evidence which suggests to some degree that Strauss was in collusion with Borden, who wrote the November 1953 letter that triggered the Oppenheimer security hearing.[181]

She has also made the case that, following that letter, Strauss was probably behind Eisenhower's 'blank wall' directive to separate Oppenheimer from nuclear secrets.[182]

Even Strauss's smaller deceptions, such as concocting an excuse to publish the transcript of the Oppenheimer security hearing even though witnesses had been promised their testimony would remain secret, rebounded against him.

As for Oppenheimer – the first to leave the field – his reputation goes from strength to strength. The latest biography of him has the main title 'American Prometheus' – which is a step up from 'portrait of an enigma', after all.[183] *American Prometheus* won the

---

[179] Ken Young (2013), 'The Hydrogen Bomb, Lewis L. Strauss and the Writing of Nuclear History'. *Journal of Strategic Studies*. Vol 36, No 6: 815-840. Available at: 10.1080/01402390.2012.726924. S2CID 154257639.

[180] Young & Schilling (2019), 133-143.

[181] Priscilla Johnson McMillan (2005). *The Ruin of J. Robert Oppenheimer and the Birth of the Modern Arms Race*. New York: Viking, 73, 175-176, 301n9, 301n13.

[182] McMillan (2005), 302n7.

[183] Titles and subtitles of Bird & Sherwin (2005) *American*

Pulitzer Prize and there is a biopic on the way.

As the Oppenheimer reputation rises, so Strauss falls – though it is arguably good to be played by Robert Downey Junior. But in the two decades since the death of Teller, his reputation is also overshadowed by the growing reputation of his great rival.

Though Oppenheimer, however exasperated he was with Teller, would have been the first to recognise that Teller's research skills were in many ways superior to his own.

Teller's ability to raise money in Washington was second to none. But we may not know how far he really managed to get with his third-generation nuclear project until the time comes – by which time it will probably be too late for all of us.

The H-bomb is a nuclear weapon a thousand times as powerful as the bombs that devastated Hiroshima and Nagasaki. Such ordinary fission bombs would henceforth be regarded as small tactical nuclear weapons. By 1986, the USA had 23,317 nuclear weapons and the USSR had 40,159. By early 2019, more than 90 percent of the world's 13,865 nuclear weapons were owned by the United States and Russia.

Nine nations now have nuclear weapons.

On 7 July 2017, more than 120 countries voted to adopt the UN Treaty on the Prohibition of Nuclear Weapons. Elayne Whyte Gómez, President of the UN negotiations on the nuclear ban treaty, said: "The world has been waiting for this legal norm for 70 years," since the atomic bombings of Hiroshima and Nagasaki in August 1945.

In the end, Oppenheimer was a sensitive man who expressed himself carefully and often obscurely – as he did during his brave visit to Japan with Kitty in 1960. Asked by reporters if he felt sorry about his role in the bombing, he said: "I do not regret that I had something to do with the technical success of the atomic bomb. It

---

Prometheus: The Triumph and Tragedy of J Robert Oppenheimer. New York: Knopf; and Bernstein (2004) *Oppenheimer: Portrait of an enigma,* London: Duckworth. What a difference a year makes..!

isn't that I feel bad. It is that I don't feel worse tonight than I did last night."[184]

That is a wonderful example of clarity, mixed with obscurity, a combination at which Oppenheimer excelled. It also gives the impression of depth.

**

Oppenheimer seems great to us now because he wrestled with his conscience and peered into the future. He was very influenced in this by Niels Bohr – who had a meeting with Churchill at the end of the war even more disastrous than Oppenheimer's meeting with Truman. Churchill did not agree with Bohr that openness was going to be vital in international nuclear politics and tried to persuade Roosevelt to have him arrested – in case he took it upon himself to tell the Russians.

Bohr died in 1962, but he consistently believed in the importance of openness and honesty as the way forward – for scientists and for the technology they created.

It was not until the British Marxist historian E. P. Thompson founded European Nuclear Disarmament (END) in 1980, with its idea of 'détente from below', that openness between the sclerotic politics of East and West was forged into a weapon that could be used to bring peace.

Even so, Oppenheimer foresaw clearly the dangers of secrecy with nuclear weapons.

These days, we are as far away as ever from handing over all our nuclear materials to any international body overseeing all things nuclear – perhaps even further than when Truman flirted with the idea in 1946.

Yet once more we are threatened by nuclear disaster thanks to Vladimir Putin and his invasion of Ukraine.

It may be time, given that, that we looked once more at the story of the great pioneers of nuclear weapons.

---

[184] Goodchild (1980), 274.

Printed in Great Britain
by Amazon